In This Nightmare I'm Living In

Parts of Gregory Schlau Jr. Journals

Series One

Gregory J. Schlau Jr.

In This Nightmare I'm Living In
Parts of Gregory Schlau Jr. Journals

Copyright © 2024 by Gregory J. Schlau Jr.

Paperback ISBN: 978-1-63812-950-9
Hardcover ISBN: 978-1-63812-952-3
Ebook ISBN: 978-1-63812-951-6

All rights reserved. No part in this book may be produced and transmitted in any form or by any means, electronic, or mechanical, including photocopying, recording, or by any information storage and retrieval system, without permission in writing from the copyright owner.

The views expressed in this work are solely those of the author and do not necessarily reflect the views of the publisher. It hereby disclaims any responsibility for them.

Published by Pen Culture Solutions   05/09/2024

Pen Culture Solutions
1-888-727-7204 (USA)
1-800-950-458 (Australia)
support@penculturesolutions.com

In This Nightmare I'm Living In

by
Gregory J. Schlau Jr.

Why Don't I Know What Love Is?

Just like your life's story, mine is also full of a lot of hurting and scars that are hard to heal. When I was young to now in my 30s, I've only been a toy for so, so many women; never nothing more but just a one-night. To just keep counting my time that I feel is up with no love; to just be a one-timer; to be with women for only pleasure, nothing more, nothing else; to be with no woman; to just wanting a woman for just love, but to not or never feel what love is…

To just be a toy, a tool with no batteries for so many years of my youth to become a man who is so emotionally empty, with no one to listen, to have a heart that is now hurting, with the cards that were dealt; to not being okay with- out a pure, true love. To be for every night drowning in this cold shower with these tears that just keep running down this cold face of mine, wishing for more than being used, feeling my life is around this barbed-wire, feeling I'm guilty of not being more of what women want, to not being looked at for more. A man with this heavy heart, I'm feeling like I'm not to be a just a broken- down car that just gets used for a ride; for me it may take a while to understand that, for it to hurt; to feel it in my chest; to miss what was. I never had in this life to not let go of something I never held; to know if I get my calling, it would not because of my health. That is not going well, with cancer, with life going down, with this fake smile, with hurting more to keep saying "If I go, it will be because of a broken heart." No doctors, no one can heal; being so scared of being in this, brokenness with no other reason but a heart that's not having it anymore. With my health getting harder, with a heart with so much pain I wish I could regret that I can't get away from it; to feel it - will never be okay with it not being right for so many that don't care to love, to abuse it, for so many that don't care for me to live in a struggling nightmare where I live. It what's making me to be dying slowly with so much pain, bearing me alone with a heart that's not pumping right. No more to keep asking, "Why is he doing this?" Pain, begging, praying, for him, every night, for my forgiveness; to stop this agony, watching my days go by with me where can't stop crying, wishing I could of have a love with me to have a life before I fly away. Time is just against me, knowing I will never be number one in this world of love with nothing left of me; to just have memories that just fade of so many women I slept with; to not have no woman to save me from this situation I'm going through with so much pain. With this hurt feeling, I can't get back up, with my paranoia with my life, manipulating me to start having P.T.S.D. to fight, to find a love; being scared of having no one to try to help me out of this pain I'm in. To just be in love for my own heart; to feel better; to now feel it being gone up this wall with truth broken, with no love of a feeling of it. For me, with feeling I'm nothing, but I have silence in my chest, being scared of if can make it through this; if can make it in my life with pain, I never felt knocking in my body, shaking, bearing me, having cancer running around me. Please, don't worry about this; it's not no one's fault but my own for me thinking I was more than a toy. If I was ever to fall in love, to now see I'll just never get any closer in this life that's closing in, on me, and getting tighter, to just wish it was a dream, to wish my secret's lusciousness was still with me to hold me with a little love, to being wishing she was here. To get the honor to talk to her last night; to wish she lived by me. When I talked to her last night, it just brings back so many memories we had, knowing I was just a tool, but knowing I couldn't never do better, now my heart's feeling it when she's so far. Even if it was so many years ago, I was starting to feel something I had never felt in my life with her. Now so far from me, with me to want to try something new, as loving only her, it's now always echoing in my head with this aching to see her; gone and so many before now gone from me. To be lucky that I had them, but to wish more than lust and more than love is to say this, I never wanted to say, but they're better, probably better without me. All my life, it wasn't me while women stand there with their eyes always on me, not looking away from me, for me to be looking at an angel with horns; for them to not be looking for the long term; for them to be knowing I will treat them as queens while I'm not feeling any wrongs or guilty, or a crime with that ring on their fingers. I'm about to go with them feeling so sweet with this tenderness while they're having a sweet tooth for me while they keep blinking their eyes, feeling we can do more than being friends, when I can see they want to feel me with love, but lust for only a sun to go down. This rising feeling, A feeling so hot, so wet, having so much strength for more time with as my brain cells to just keep running while she's taking me away from this life. Even if it's only a night, knowing this is a life being so used to be in to putting a smile on their faces while they're showing me their appreciation of just being their toy, only a tool of life, of lust; and no more, or nothing else; and even not knowing what was, but I still it's in my chest that I have never had before. No one will feel it unless you were just nothing but a tool; nothing more with over a hundred women to losing it to, not what it is if you never had it before!

On August 17, 2006, three days before my twenty-first birthday, I get hit by a - semi, losing all. That same day, I went into a coma. I lost a woman of lust that I loved that starting sleeping with another girl; then losing my football scholarship that I worked so hard for; and getting cancer in a blood transfusion in surgery of when the doctors did brain surgery on me. It took 14 years for a doctor to find I had bone marrow disease from that surgery in August 2006. that has no cure, but to take a pint of blood out every two weeks for the rest of my life...

We Need More Uniting

An hour and a half ago, I had to fight a seizure, my epilepsy; I won the other three this week, Knowing If I die, it will not because of weaknesses, not because of lack of courage, or not being strong enough. It's going to be because I'm broken, how my life is, with so much hatred. In our society, families, friends, and garages, when families, Communities, and the... world should be more united, with love more, with peace, to try to put our hatred Beside us, and all try to stick more together, to never hold on to it Before it's too late. When someone's always going to be hurt until their living days, to put all aside With Our lives being too short. To love, honor with support; To try become more as uniting, never not to bare one out; To always cherish and hold one another; To never let go of how life is so short. With only one life, try to respect it. I have many crowded pains in this chest, having no lover or a friend, having no.... buddy to fight at night, just to lie here alone, oh, with so much pain in my heart, having no hugging or kissing, to just sitting in this cold raining night, hoping for more. Instead, there are lonely nights in this bed, knowing what it feels like with this so-broken angel; I have cancer running my life without a love or a friend to help me through so many raining days, to believe it I can't stop trying even when I'm dying inside with my hourglass almost gone so empty, with my tears so gone, and there's nothing anybody can do...

Tearing Me

I feel I need a psychiatrist or someone to help; I'm feeling like I'm hearing voices of my once loved one going, drowning me without her, tearing me apart. My heart won't let her go, wishing for her, lying here in my room, crying for her, and needing someone to save me from so much agony. Being so young, not having no love, having gone far without, only to hurt. How is it possible to not have the only one I loved? To be living above me, without me, to save her; to - come home, feeling so alone; to always feel it's raining around me. Three hundred forty-five days of cold showers, not being okay, waking up with tears rolling down, this hurting heart feels it every morning. I can't get away from it because I loved them too much; having no one to wipe these cold tears in my life, to be honest with myself, I can't breathe from this thing breaking into shattering pain. I'm sure I am dying slowly without love, feeling so guilty of my first love, wishing I could still have her watching; tears rolling on her picture.

On Fire So Lost

My life is darkness; every day, every second, I can't breathe; trying not to let go; feeling I died; just seeing nothing but red, so when I close my eyes, I'm not ready for heaven calling me. Pain, having no future in this dark life; having so much broken, it can't heal without help. Help me through these tears, all because I can't love like I'm supposed to with every night feeling so alone, having no love beside me. I'm hanging around to hear this ring tone, to hear your vice one more time. It hurts really bad, not having you, but to lose you in my life, it doesn't feel like nothing can work out. My love not being around me; to be alone, it hurts the most to lose my heart. I needed you the most in August 17. I lost more than my pride; I lost a love and got new blood that barely helped me, but to give me cancer that's now running through me like water flowing in rivers. As I want to disappear, fading in this darkness of pain, loosening everything but my life. I pray, "why?" I didn't deserve it. It hurts me more when I look next to me, not having nothing but this tear rolling with no ending; young, having no love, having a chance to, but lose it all when I got struck by this 18- wheeler, to always up waiting for my once love. Come to me, to be airtight with more love. I can't control what I have for this life; to be here all alone without love, my life is so upside down.

This broken road, with me feeling always blue, with it being so hard, feeling it in my heart, I can't go on with my life that is on fire; so lost. There is so much darkness, I'm in. To ask, "Is this real?" I lost my whole world being hurt, trying to hide it so much. Even my smile that's so fake is hurting so much inside. Every day, I cry myself empty, so weak, turning cold without no love; having nothing to give anymore.

I feel, I live in a river with my tears, Feeling all alone, having no one, Not being perfect but I'm trying, Feeling my need in to find a love, I believe I'm always in a struggle that drives me crazy with my mind, with my hoping for a true love, Making me feel I'm not wanted, Always hurting inside with pain that never stops....

Turning Cold

I'm always so full of love; to have no love, I can't find myself. I'm so deeply feeling so alone with so much anticipation to find someone real to watch this sunrise with it starting to fade farther in this dark night, feeling so empty, weak, turning cold without no love, thinking it was too late, making it so things that go wrong in my life with no love. With destiny fading more this night, crying late, wishing I could see her again. I'm so cold with having no one, where no one will help feeling so alone, having so much love to be broken...

Dear Roswell Cancer Institute

Hello,

I'm GREGORY J SCHLAU JR.,

A writer and author in poetry,

For every one of my books or eBooks I sell, I will donate 10% percentage of my earnings to your cancer institution.

Every year, the money will go back into my private foundation and then back to you.

I hope to have two books out every year. For fifteen years,

Thank you for your services and help saving my life and millions more than me.

Much love sent to you all!

Thanks for giving me hope in this second life....

– Author Gregory J. Schlau Jr.

My Heart Feeling Broken

My heart is stuck in rewind, with my love. Ending: feeling It's gone, and crying is the only light I have with no velvet or no love anymore. With So little life left, When I am by myself, looking for my own; To IT, end short, Being so blind. I can't listen to my own Heart; to it's never Healing right. Now, being so lost, I have no love to be alone, having just In a Long Nightmare; being single; For the rest of My life, feeling it Won't Be right. My First Love is gone and has Took in pieces of me with her....

Love Before

I close my eye, having visions of my life ending short, like my dad trying to stand up once more, holding my own experience, always getting back up; with so much pain, being in denial, every day, it's breaking me, having so many telling me I'll never make it anywhere. Growing up on this Eastside will make you or break you in so many pieces if you don't stand in place staying in your own lane. Having cancer, my life is on its last string; to be alone having just been crucified, wishing I had a chance to be a good man through this rest of life. My love, having so many in this life, to end it in pain with no one else to be with, I wish I could go on with a love. For this Lord to be hurting me; to be alone, heartless, without love being in an addiction, I have to try to find love before I die alone, having nothing As I never seen this coming, my heart in this dirt too heavy to pick back up, feeling so empty with no love for my heart, feeling lost without no... help having no reasons for me to love again, or even if I do, I need to make my seed to bloom; spread my legacy to give life a meaning; to grow having my name grow when my time's ending. I'd be happy to know my blood is growing to help this planet love each other, to not erase peace or serenity; to not despair....

Can't Breathe Without Her

I'm so lonely feeling like I'm nothing when I'm all alone, feeling so one of a kind, so broken, I'm Aching in denial, having no one else to save me from this hurt. While I lie here, nothing seems to be okay; falling apart, being one and only, always crying myself to tossing, turning, twisting, sweating. All nights can't sleep; I can't breathe, needing some oxygen for someone to please help me. With love being one of a kind, an addiction, why I'm asking for help; to be in a rehabilitation; praying for help to get out. This hurt, I never felt before. One love, now gone, hurting, feeling it. When I take a breath in, I turn blue; Having no love, feeling my life isn't full without someone else with me; To be without true, pure love, it hurts, to be used to being hurt, so broken inside I'm waiting alone, cold, being obsessed with love; being in addiction to hurt when all alone I have nothing to hold through so many raining nights. In the shower, hoping for love to fulfill my hurt, so many nights now - cold, holding my pillows, looking for a woman who loves me for me, without being just friends. I have so many nights of just wanting more; for the right one to come with full heart, even when I try and fall; to be getting back to find true love, even if it really hurts....

A Victim

I'm up waiting so alone, raining in my room with this dead night, crying for hope that glued me in this cold life. With me being so numb with pain in my heart, never to heal, I feel like a victim of so much pain because I can't love like I'm supposed to. With every breath I take with this pain, I wish I wasn't a convict, stealing so many hearts; to be a loner is my biggest fear; to always be emptying my tears on a roller-coaster, never knowing where I am; so lonely, a broken angel sent to hell for a living; to have never loved again.

Never Fall into Love Ever Again

The only fear I always have is to never fall into love ever again, having so many nights crying, wishing I could have just one more chance in this life; one more time in love. No one knows how I felt, wishing I could be with someone every night, feeling love, having gone far without reaching for a life; to wish I can fall in love, hold someone, not this pillow that keeps getting wet. My heart keeps interfering with mind; every second I breathe, I'm drowning with- out a love in my tears at night, feeling like nothing matters; to always end on my mattress; to always try and find something where I will always try my best to be alone. I think of you," " my love", even if it's been year's ago, I can't get you out of my mind; hoping you can hear me; I'm crying out, for someone to save me. Lately, I can't stop thinking of you ") (being the only one; for you being a last call, just know I feel so alone here without your input. My one and only love, wishing I could still hold you on these raining nights, begging for one more night to get me out this blue dark room, not saying my goodbye. To turn my back Crying, wishing I never changed like these seasons, being so cold to being once heated to raining Nights. It's hard to live a life feeling so dark, being so difficult, losing someone who is close. Losing Them hurts inside, feeling life split right to the bottom, knowing there's no way to reach the top, feeling I can't hold my breath anymore. Drowning in this cold, Pain so close enough to my heart, Feeling the cracks breaking every day, I struggle with my life; I bear so much that I can't get away from me, so I don't want to be feeling the knife in my chest, trying not cry. That's why I do it inside with my fake smile, lying to you, losing my tears in hurt, waiting for the phone to ring once more before the end is near, coming with my brain cells just Running, My mind spinning, My body so numb,

Letting my heart just bleed, Being so tired to move on, Feeling I'm all by myself, so much alone, So weak, Not wanting to go through this anymore. With real love hurting, feeling so much alone, I'm needing her love, wishing she is the… one I'm talking to, not letting her go, not telling her how; For her to slip away from me, I can't handle it anymore. With her love, I'm wishing I could let her not go away without her telling her I love…

Loosening My Grip

I have no love to call; they're all gone far, only to leave me here with my heart starting to break these chain's, bleeding more without them here, with me starting, with nothing to end; to begin without my best, her being alone, never getting over her, holding onto my pillows, crying, with little time to grow together. I think of her; losing her; holding her through so many nights, crying, wishing someone to hold. It's hard to find someone as real; to watch this sun go down; to the one I close with, trying fix myself in this mirror; to be good enough; to be alone. I didn't know what love was till I lost it. I didn't know this was love until I was alone trying to hold on....

I'm loosening my grip. My heart aches every night, waiting for a chance of love that I'm so scared, knowing that I have to stand in front once again, before it's too late, to have a seed, to bloom my legacy, to make more seeds in our world where - living, knowing time's ticking in my chest. For a chance to be in a relationship with a woman who cares for me, to give her the rest of my heart, feeling it being so long, as uniting her love, I'm wishing I could still have a love before I'm gone to help me with these tears that to need to be wiped. I don't get no more phone calls from my love. To have nothing but this; to show me hurting with this pain; to stop; to have only have her back, every time, ticking off my heart and feeling so much alone without her by side.

I'm dropping to my knees, crying, wishing I could still be in her life, hugging, kissing, through a phone To just hear nothing on the other side when I pick up this phone; to have her always on my mind; to lose part of me when I lost her; to not love no one else but my once love and wishing her love, wishing her to be my number one before I die. With my life ending short, having cancer, to always have her in my heart it'd keep my life a float....

To Face with My Once Loved One

My worst day of loving someone is the day that I lost them forever. To just see her only at night where she is always shining down from the sky, where I always watch her face every time, looking for her, only to be alone and having nothing but hurt with no remorse of the pain. To be lonely in this life with a hollow chest in this big bed alone, cold, I wish I had her one more time before I lost her, for every day of my life with no end of being alone, I have nothing to love again, feeling it's impossible to be with the one I know. I couldn't do better without her, and we can't live our separate ways with me being too much in love, with it to end, being it didn't last and being so lost, so scared I'll never get to be able to live with all this pain. I live without her too. have a broken heart, never being face to face... with my once loved one. Mama, please don't cry. I just woke up from this coma; It's hard to walk to you with chains on my legs that are hurting. Mama, I promise I will try to be with you until my last days; I know it will take time to heal this body. Mama, with my broken bones, praying to our Lord, please, Help heal me; not being strong for you, my Mama, I know it will take time to learn what our life was, To know I will not be okay, Hurting, knowing I can't leave you here alone on this planet. Mama, I can't stop crying, watching you breaking down watching me as I'm dying slowly with my time being cut in half. I'm sorry this almost coasted me, my life with all you have taught me. Mama, my heart is aching with my life being so hard with these health problems I'm having, as I'm Praying to our Lord to give me remorse with mercy; I love my life, With the rest of my time so slow, battling every day to see you, my mama. I will not give up on you, my mother. I love you so much;

to do that to you, as I'm trying to hold on, even if I'm hurting every second, we are living....

Dear First Love That's Now Anonymous

The more I try, the more I fall; I knew after that day that I could never move on. My love is falling in her spell; I'm not sure if I can find my way out. I'm Sorry For not being able to make Our Wishes come true. My dear friend, my dear first love That's now Anonymous, Ominous Love That will always make me smile.

I'M TRYING TO HOLD ON

I'm trying to hold on, but my time is slow; I don't know how long sorry go with nothing easing my mind with the pain, losing my dear little brother to the sky, asking for strength to try to keep my composure With so much pain I can't get rid of, Not feeling right to be hurting. Every night, I have visions when I close my eyes, dreaming of our once memories, with my life, with so much darkness trying to find lighter, I feel I can't breathe with so much agony in my life; to be lying in hurt, wishing for my little brother in my life...

Drowning

I feel nobody loves me like she did. I couldn't get over of the life; I can't pretend I can't get over her. With love and hate of this pain, I can't sleep; I will never be the same. My heart really needs her. To try to get by myself where the streets keep calling my mind, I'm losing my heart. It feels so tired; it just keeps falling in pain. My head is not going to be with you, but to be alone with so much emotional scarring, crying, to have no more love. To be over her, holding onto my beginning, I'm dying slow down this broke road without her, not having real, so real love. She was the one and only one I tried to love. To be alone just so I hurt some more; to be broken with no one being more perfect than my angel. Every time I fall asleep, she gets to be with me. Fading, my love disappearing, I'm so lost with feeling my love having gone, crying, writing; in my head, I can't breathe. I'm drowning without her here. To be with the one who I love a lot; to darken my life without her love...

When Losing My Love

It hurts the most to see we had to go our separate ways. I never told how much she meant, holding her picture close by me every day, breaking me into pieces with so much hurt. It puts me out of commission, losing my mind, lining to myself to walk around with a fake smile and with something inside me: this pain. Having no future, having my guard down, to lose my love I know everybody falls in love. For me not to keep filling up, to fall in love, not being a crime to try to love for a long time, to just get hurt by love that's not even there; there isn't no joy in this life without a love hugging me through these troubling times in my life. I'm only trying to hide it from the heart, but it won't fill without true love. It hurts in this life; why couldn't love find me meaningful, with my heart bleeding with no end in sight? Will I die without love? Please, I know, please save me; I'm lonely, broken, lost…

myself, looking for love. I can't forget the pain in my chest, being trapped in this nightmare, Not knowing what's my wrong, being scared of my life going on a wild horse, knowing my life cost me time to get back up. Crying, wishing I could still have a better chance of living, Feeling I'm guilty for not trying, riding out this tornado, rain that won't stop crying, feeling so bad for my heart, feeling like I can't breathe from this agony of my life. I bear writing my life, I bear my own feelings, for my heart feels so much alone in my chest; That comes from this situation, for my time that goes slowly in pain; To have visions in these nightmares of this Semi hitting me, a cell with these chains; I can't get off my life. To have my freedom back that I bear it with, it hurts inside with my time ending slowly. I'm always going to fight to my end, to be around my life, Even more it breaks; Me again, I'm going try to hold on until my afterglow, to try to find love with peace; Serenity in the world we live in. For me to find my other piece, to put this love story into a being, to stop with the fake, but to mean this smile, Walking with this head to the sky, … Never looking down, …

To have a little one before my time runs out, without me, for my heart to feel love once again With No Warning, I just sometimes want to give it up; this life's not treating me right. To feel I'm always IN wrong, trying to walk away, leaving me bleeding, always starting over, my heart always getting colder and having no one to hear my cry. I'm trying to be strong, to give a reason to keep my purpose of life, not knowing how much longer I'll hold onto a life that's always breaking me to my knees, praying for more hope to glue this heart together. Missing pieces, I'm starting to fade away, and next to the light, closing my eyes, I'm hoping I see the sun rise with no end. I have no velvet love, so little life left to be alone, just so. I hurt so many nights, crying, wishing for some more nights where I find a true love before it's too late, making me sad. Without a love in my corner, every night; can't stop believing in my life, feeling broken, always crying myself empty; never full and having so much P.T.S.D A As I lay here so much alone wearing all black, Having no help to save me ....

To No End

I lost my heart; it's just not beating. My mind's racing like a roller-coaster, never knowing where I'm going to end no matter what I did, but just lose it all. When I want to give all up with this pain to face it, my life's ending slowly, painful; hoping to be able to hold a loved one to show me what's next in my life. My life is feeling broken being without, but with this pain, I'm losing all hope for real love; with this life, I'm living with so much wrong, not having much to be but alone with paranoia. So please, someone help me; my life is so impossible to live, even when at my loneliest. I feel I'm living in hell like; to have no one hear me in my life; to be honest; to try finding love, Blaming myself, With my eyes being so cloudy, Being so intoxicated, in denial when I can't find pure love with time that is ticking, and I'm Dying so slow without having love....

Cold Night

When I lie, I close my eyes, wishing I didn't live this life with so much going down, falling from this floor, praying for the strength, scared of love, scared I'll never put my arms around another love while I stare up at this cold night, feeling the Lord is about to get me on indictment while I cry. Feeling so tired on the bottom of this darkness just to be a loner, going in this dark shadow closely hitting my heart with love, for this love to be disappearing, fading in this trap, that hurts me more when I say I loved to be almost at my end with no love; to be alone, having nothing to hold through so many nights, I cried cold.....

Someone I'm Lucky to Had Have in This Life

This is to my little brother; I wish you were here walking with me, feeling like we never had a full life. To begin without you, feeling so lost, losing you, my little brother, IT'S Putting me in this cold numb night, crying late, hoping to see you again, having so much to talk about, like this cancer that's running through me. To laugh again of our memories that are not fading away from me, I love you, my little brother. Always makes cry; without you, my heart folded in half with so much pain. Being in denial, every day, I stare at your picture. It's the only thing I have left of us. Now we are apart; I can't stop crying, bear lying, and breathing right now. I lost you, my little brother, I wish I could still have you here. Love you always, my little brother, this is not goodbye, I will always be looking in this cold sky. As my ... days are closing in my fear, with me falling to the floor drowning, to try to swim back every day; fighting to stay up in this flood, knowing my mission isn't complete. Even if I'm crying inside, to say with my end, I tried to fight my health to be with in my life, to hope I'd find a love by my side; to give a spark; to bring back my heart feeling so alone, hoping it can be fixed before Old Faithful calls my name. I'm thinking of this - every night in my chest, and it hurts to be the only one...

My One and Only Grandmother

To my one and only grandmother, who I love a lot, even if I really don't remember half our lives together, I do know what I know now. How you remind so much to me in my life, knowing how lucky I am to be your grandson, wishing I could go back in time to remember what is missing in my mind and feeling so much is lost. I know you have a heart that's made from the finest, purest love and wisdom, surely and sprinkle as its years unfold with your heart that goes on like a sweet garden of rare beauty, being thoughtful to others sincerely as a duty in life with as precious of rare flowers surely always so sweet. A treasure of God's to help other flowers in this world bloom to all, so sincere, you, my lovely grandmother...

No Love Far

I've been in pain; I want to live and try to keep my head up. I do this by myself, having no help fixing this heart beating, knowing that I can't answer from the sky. Waiting for me to be next, watching time tick away, caring if I was saving my life, going under, having nothing but hurt and dying slow with no help, with no one else; having no one to lessen so much under pressure, saying it so many times: I need someone to save me when I close my eyes, swearing I don't want to see this life I'm living with so many having a no more heart on fire. I am not sure how to love again with my heart; just pain, having no future in my head, spinning, drowning without a love in stress, giving me no more time....

Having no princess

I wish I had found something before this time passes away from my life, not meaning nothing without the one. I'm having so many regrets that I never get to be with my love. Having so much pain, how do I live without no love in my life, having no time to restore this name to its fullness; to be watching time go without having - no one to help me up and to stare at this broken mirror, always watching these tears freeze. To feel I'm losing hope to find true love, being so young having no princess to save me; having no morning shine in this dark moment in this nightmare; feeling so empty with so much silence on my mind. Hating that every second I'm to be alone, as I am starting to lose and tweaking, as I'm starting to hear but not seek; as my heart is still bleeding. My mom, I'm so sorry seeing you crying, watching those tears rolling on your face, my lovely mom, I will always try to hold on, but it's hard to walk with these shackles on my feet, being chained to be losing someone we loved. Please, our Lord, have mercy. Please give my mother more strength to handle this pain, to be wishing life wasn't so much. Aching, hurting, I know you're aching in your heart, and it isn't right, losing someone we care so much about. Please Let me help wipe your tears that're raining so hard where we have no power with this storm in our lives, Mother, I know it's hard, but please don't cry; life is a battle of our love going on. There's so much cold water; let's stick - together to keep ourselves warm with these storms in our lives. To my dear mom I love so deeply, feeling our life is so short to try to love every moment, every day, every night we have left for you to please hold on what we have left...

Without you here

I have locked myself in the bathroom on the cold floor, begging prayerfully to remember What's it's feels like to fall in love, sitting, bleeding hurting alone, I can't lose hope when I can't breathe, being so weak. Having no one to hear my cry with my love so gone, being so sour, begging for love at least one more, it's tearing me, knowing my love is fading away from me, knowing this love driving me losing it in my head. For so many nights crying, I can't get over love wishing; Some way, I can find my true love lying here alone, it hurts more, not living right, not letting love go; it hurts, wishing I could have still had one chance to fall in love. It's hard to always be in the dark, not knowing what is to be in the light or what it feels like to have a love, but to let it fade to an erase....

If I'm in Pain

My life Is Always putting me at set back; I can't get over with the words, to be always in my heart will always echoing, to always try to fall forward, to always fall in a bad day That turns in a dark cloud. To try face it, always try to step forward, to try to win, never lose, to learn to never forget, what's always trying to break me with the pain that is temporary, and know it's not permanent, to know how much you are going through, there is no limit on never giving up, even though the - impossibly. From my own experience, always getting back up With so much pain to get stronger, to always get ready to fight and face any situation that comes, to always move forward in my multiversity of pain That always makes me crawl to make an impact in my life. If I save a life or beat cancer, Over a love, To learn my life is no game For just living, To never give up, To always get on with life Where There's light with uniting, To struggle To get back up With a full heart, even if I feel there is no reason to go any more, To try self-love, To Try not self-hatred With Life being short, To try make a difference in it, Even if I'm in pain ....

Feeling everything is crumbling

I feel these walls are closing in while I'm sitting in these dark, cold showers of my life. I'm aching in always asking forgiveness for my heart that's having so many different things going on when - I don't know if I can get rid of it with it always echoing on fire. I'm NOT going to let this dream go like everything else that's been taken from me. I know I can make mistakes, and I will learn from them knowing it will take time, I know. I have so many things that go wrong with me having seizures and cancer, but to try live every moment, I have left knowing life is no game. I always try to give it my all when I'm writing every day, having no joking, to always be struggling, to always work hard where I feel my mission will never be complete, not finding my true love to be. Every night when I cry, praying I find someone special before my time is up, I always try to love with no hatred, to find happiness, or if it exist to always try to show love for them to turn their backs, for it seems it never changes; every night holding my pillows, crying to try to understand knowing no one wants to be alone, knowing it's not fair wishing my life wasn't real, being scared knowing one day when I close my eyes, I might not or never see my sunrise when flying away with no love beside me, being so - lost that I tried to love with it almost being too late...

I'm trying to breathe, but it keeps getting caught

Why do I keep doing this to myself? For me, not being okay, for me always waking, feeling I can't move on, feeling I'm so in denial of my life always, echoing on fire. I'm not going anywhere in pain to be wiped away from it, so I can't breathe from this agony. I have to say that I don't know how I can find a way to get back to my own mind, spinning out of control, feeling I need a doctor to help me; as I'm dying slowly with my life ending up with nothing. I'm feeling this cancer; I can't believe I have to be alone with no love, feeling this depression in my chest, having no one when I cry for some oxygen at night, wishing I had some- one to remember me. Please, give me Mercy. I care if I live or die to have a son, not I need; I'm running out tears to cry As I lie here feeling love gone, so Scared, I don't know what it means, Knowing it isn't easy to be here alone, Wishing for a love to - remember, With a heart so broken, Every night, Starring out this cold window, Needing someone, Here at least one more night, Before my time runs out, To try with the rest of my strength, To hold on for a love that will stay at least once more. To be not feeling this heart beating, to just hear her say, "Baby, I love you, Baby, I'll never leave you," To hear, "I can't imagine this world without you," Hopping with no more silence beside me....

My Life Feeling So Dark

I'm up waiting for love, waiting for her even though I know this takes time for her to come home. Feeling so alone having no more heart, dying so slow, if it's a drug that controls my mind every time I fall, she hypnotizing my love, thinking I was in love. To know I need rehabilitation going though withdraw, I hope I find real love, feeling so rich of love, to feel it's just not real to not have no love to hold you through the night; to hold nothing but this wet pillow late through so many raining nights, hoping it's no longer and hoping I run in to love again, acting like it doesn't hurt to have no love - to hold me tight through my life. With this pain my in life, to have cancer running through me alone with this, I'm in; I can't stop. With my scars, I was hoping they didn't show. I hope for real love. Is this too late? Without love, to be falling alone. Please wake me up, out this nightmare, to be again with love, to be out of my heart, and not have a lock on it. For me to be losing my feelings, for love gone; to be on a long road with so many holes broken into my life, being in the worst pain I ever had. To be feeling the only thing I can hold is this wet pillow, feeling like a heart attack given all love to be empty. To cry, sober, being in the worst pain I ever felt in my chest, all I try to hold on to is finding love, wishing for a rehab to treat my pain. It's not being easy on my own, being so alone in this world we are in. I tried so many nights, bleeding, hurting so lost. Is it too late to have love, thinking I can't be part of someone's heart and feeling it was an act of my life to make. It hurts inside with pain in the dark, not being able or still being able to get back up, to drown in this cold, not finding true, pure love; trying to earn her - love, praying for her love me back....

Cardinals

As I sit here smoking a cigarette, knowing I'm hearing chirping getting louder, it just won't stop being so cold in the morning. The chirping took me outside to see it was a red cardinal, who I think is my little brother, thinking he's still beside me. To go speak to him, tell him I love him, thank him for still being here with me. I'm not feeling so alone as he comes and checks on me once in a while...

Hurting on Christmas

I miss the person who I was when we first met; even when I never switched it up, I always stood by your love. It's a lot to take in. With this love we had, there was So much trust, in our lives, wishing for, being in love again, Once more holding you, in this world, being So warm, My - heart always pumping. Now, waiting alone by this Christmas tree, with your gift, waiting up for me to just be alone. Having no one on this... Christmas night, crying late, holding your gift, hoping you would show; Hurting, spending Christmas alone, without you, Love having gone to leave me here alone, with my heart bleeding, With No warning, it hurts more. I can't let you go. Being so broken in this mirror, watching my tears roll away from you, my love, Christmas Can't be without you. My heart will never start again, not having your love on this Christmas night...

My Life with No Love Ending

It's just not the same, my life, with no love ending. While I was young, I felt this pain, My Life with No Love Ending, it's just not the same, my life, with no love ending. While I was young to feel this pain, Alone, having fallen to her arms, To this night's end. Without her love, because I'm so not ready to be alone, having - fallen to her arms, to this night's end. Without her love, I'm so not ready to move On. She'll be...

My life; Without her, it's Tearing me apart; My heart so on fire. So lost, so badly that I was not able to hold her until her ending. Why can I not move? My cold heart, feeling so sad That my want for true love is gone, filled with sadness the more I cry. When The one I loved Is gone, There isn't no going back to fix it, Knowing That I can't stop loving her for a living; To have nothing but this hurt that won't go on without her, My only love...

Is It Really in My Head?

I can't trust no one, It's really my head; I don't think I can love any more, having so much pain in my thoughts of the one I loved. My life changed from lust overnight to making love, never getting to hold you again. It's hard; It's always cold, and losing your love makes this dark shadow that follows me every night that's gone by. I can't get over you, my precious Angel of love, having walked these streets alone, growing older, I'm all alone without you, my Love, we had even more. I'm not sure how much I can hold onto. Coming home to find you not there, I feel my heart will never be the same without you…

My dear Sofia

I miss you; where are you? I'm at my end. It's so close to my life going on fire, so lost. So long, it seems I just lost you. To be alone without you, my wounds are just bleeding; love can't be fixed. Crying, you left without me; to be hurting, knowing you can't be replaced; there was only one I ever loved. For you to be gone for so long, it's never ending with this pain. Every time I close these eyes, hoping to wake up from this dream where in my life is feeling broken, that's good enough for love when I know it's a drug, an addiction I could never overcome. Without you, it's destroying me, suffocating, choking; I can't breathe, drowning; my heart so broken, my love, Sofia. I have no one to listen; my heart won't let her go. Wishing I could have just been out of here, to disappear, fading away from love, drowning; can't wait for her, only to be without you. I am so lost, walking around as an angel without his wings. To face this hurt without her with me, drowning; I can't swim with these tears. Sadly, I can't stop loving her; baby, I was supposed to be with you. Baby, I'm yours. Life is fading away from me, and only you can save from this hurt I have inside. As I need help; I have so much love for you. To be alone, I've just been crucified and wishing I could go back, knowing how lucky I was, saving her life, just staring down from this cold night with no water, so weak, turning into a cold night. I hear voices, but not seeing you is driving me to cry. When I have no one to save me, having P.T.S.D., crying late for someone to hear me being alone, never getting over her....

Without Your Love, I'm Dying Slow

When I've have fallen in love too early, To Know how it's so real, being young, I'm still learning and having so much I'm Running from. To wake up alone, Once holding her To Holding my pillow, losing oxygen, Wishing I've never fell in that dark hole and how much it hurts. When I lose what I've depended on the most that now is gone. With no end, Pain in my Heart, Hurt, dying Young, having no love, Having A chance for It to End short, When I've Need her the most, having cancer, Stress always on my mind, How I've Felt, Wishing I could go to her, Not knowing how much Can I take, as my Heart is being so filled with sorrow, Without her. Where is she now? Her love means so much to me, where I can't wait any longer. Dying slow with so much pain, Being in Denial, with her love that's always Makes it hurt more, having lost my love, and going down this hill face first, without her, it's not going well. Being gone too far without only to hurt more nights, Alone, crying for her, to just wait. As I'm alone, having no one to give me strength and to help me fight back this cancer that's running through my veins and just away from my calling, without love, dying so slow.

As I know everybody falls in love. But not for me, to keep filling up to fall in love, not being a crime to try to love for a long time, to just get hurt by love that's not even there isn't no joy in this life without a love hugging me through these troubling times. My life's lonely, trying to hide it from the heart won't fill without true love hurts in this life. Why couldn't love find me meaningful with my heart bleeding with no end in sight or die without love? I know, please, save me I'm lonely, broken, as I lost myself looking for love...

A Missed Love Feeling Like a Dog Pound

My love, you are gone; My life feels like a dog pound, crying for you, waiting to come back in to my life; That's going on without you to save me from always feeling so alone, crying late, trying to let myself go from what we had, Fading, almost is gone. Having Nothing, being so alone, crying, trying to be strong enough to miss. What we had wasn't no fantasy of losing you; It feels like it's always raining ever since the I last saw you, holding you through so many nights. Now Cold, holding onto what's left of my heart, lying under me right now, under this cold window at Night where I can't stop calling for you. To hear your voice in this room where I'm dying - without you, my love is a curse. You're always on my mind. With so much hurt, to say this Is good bye, or where our story ends…

Silence of Love

I just want to make this work; Life, for me, feels like living in darkness, constantly in pain When I checked out. When My Love Died out Of This life, Leaving Me Alone; When I know I deserved her to end up With Nothing Hurting the Most. When Her picture was lost, fading, to only, to have her love in this cold heart, losing my best friend, someone I'll always miss. Where she slept every night, Missing Her kiss missing to say Goodnight, my love, With Nothing but Her silence Where I'm breaking, my heart Being mistaken of a love that's Now gone…

She Left So Me Empty

As she left me empty and weak without her. With most of my days being so gray, I wish I could say something to you with all my problems, I hope we can solve them. I don't want to give others my heart to bleed more out; My heart isn't the same without you I'm so scared; I don't have the strength; so, scared I don't have you, always having it rain on me. Always Smoking like if it was legal to be alone, I would feel safe at this dark corner, crying late, I wish I could fall asleep when I wake from not having you by my side with this pressure of love Just to be blamed for it, to hurt to smoke, to release this stress is a chain of pain of sickness. In this life with no one being perfect, being unfortunate, she is the one that needed the rest; I have no - velvet to this life; I'm wishing I can change the fact; I wish I could live with this pain,

I wish I could live without you, having too much patience to try rechanging my name every day, it's breaking me to pieces with this pain; as it's just filling with anxiety without her.

Why is there So Much Hurt?

As I'm So Numb I can't realize my life, being nothing But So Much Hurt, It's Slipping away, for many nights, so scared of this life, As I'm Always in pain, and starting to be Starting to be numb; I Can't move, being So cold and heartless, having no more feeling Like a train wreck, and Scared Of being alone; I never wanted to lose Something so special. With all my loves, I always kept a little secret, Being over a hundred of them, Always on the low Where nobody will never Know, How many homes I really wrecked And Always having one under these arms, Taking advantage of love; To now be alone it hurts the most With Karma Breaking me to my knees, and Losing my composure, as I'm hoping to Have a chance to love, But not take advantage Of - karma, anymore and wish not To be alone, but To save me From so much. As I'm getting older, With No love and help repair this Heart that's bleeding slow, With So many scars Now starting to show, Wishing I had someone To save me From this nightmare I'm live In...

Broken Angel

I'm so lonely, a broken angel, Sent from above; I'm trying not to fall to my knees. I'm the one and only lonely, broken angel. Please understand; listen to my broken heart. There are so many missing pieces. Please, help me; just listen to my heart. I'm falling and fear there's no one to save me. I'm so lonely, oh broken angel sent from above; just keep looking into cold sky night, Asking forgiveness, why me, Lord? Why can't I find that special someone to fulfill my heart, to help find all of my missing pieces. I'm so lonely, oh broken angel; started hearing voices in my head: You're an amazing man, you work for the lord , " but I say " please, come and save me. I'm so lonely and broken, angel, I need someone to save me; just listen to my heart; - It's not beating right. I'm an angel trying to do nothing but find true love, that one special Woman to fulfill all my missing pieces of my heart, but I'm starting to fade, Not falling into love, having no one; by Myself, just the one and only, lonely, broken angel sent from above. I'm so lonely, please, just listen, my heartbeat, bleeding love, my heart dying slow, I'm so lonely, broken angel; Just listen to my broken heart, wishing I had her saving me; I'm falling in fear. There's no one to save me when I'm on my deep end, wishing I had a real angel now. That's lost when there aren't any more tears. I'm a loner, broken, lost in myself; being a broken angel, can't find my true love, it's driving me Crazy; I can't find all the missing pieces to fulfill. My broken angel heart that won't fill without true Love and it hurts...

Can't Fulfill by My Own Without Her

I'm so in love with you; There's isn't no road Like what we had, oh, how real love is when It Can't be fixed. Crying because I know I can't have you; I have no idea how to live without you. Where our love was so in a knot, my heart tied so tight, I can't pretend what we Had Wasn't real. Crying late, Hoping, for you where We Stopped at, Knowing I can't fulfill by my own…

Wishing I Could Hold You in the Moonlight

Watching my life go on with no end to find myself praying; is there any female out there for me? Standing here alone and in despair waiting for her; is she out there? I wish I could fall in love to find that someone that fills your heart and completes you… I just share every day as ups and downs together to… is she out there? Is she waiting for me, does she think of me? Is she looking for me? Is it in our future that we will be together as one in harmony? I have not lost hope that I will be someday with her and she with me; As I am here on this cold dark night feeling a little lost and out of control, I know Tomorrow will come, and I will be up and ready to help those in need. I'm here for a purpose; I finally see I'm here to help those to get some inspiration from me and what I've battled through in turmoil. I will not let it spoil what's ahead for you, my friend, just wait and see. One step ahead, and you, too, will see if there's light at the end of the tunnel for you and me. My heart feeling so woozy, can't stop crying, thinking I'm losing it, having no break. My love, I want to be with this pain, that being good enough here without her; Not having a side when I cry.

When I cry, not having you holding me, it's like I fall and can't get up without you. Having so many in my life, to now I have none as I lie here alone, waiting for love to just hurt more without you, to just be alone hurts the most. To not hear her voice whispering in my ear; to just have her in my head spinning, drowning in tears rolling down this broken angel. Without you, love, we had so much love. And now, as I'm being alone, always thinking I was in love, thinking you were the one, I will fall for you to be leaving me. I feel I can't breathe, trying to hide it in this dark life; being young, having no more love to not be strengthened than I have to find true love, lying in this shower, letting this water hit my face, my cheeks being so cold, holding onto nothing no more with this time to make me alone. Having no one to love me like you did, wishing I could go where you are to just now be alone; having just so much love for you, to be without your love, I can't get over you. I'm so scared I'll never get to hold you, for your love is gone far without me. To be alone, just so in love with you, there's no lie in the true love I have for you and now I'm so tired, being so broken, with my back always to the wall, to feel the darkness of hurt, but to try to get back up to always fail; To feel the pain to give up, but to feel betrayed by so many. To feel no more remorse, to have so much taken from me by an 18-wheeler, but to always get back up to be alone; To try to give up, but to have the Lord not let me Just to sit here, letting the tears roll; to ask forgiveness to the life I'm living with so much hurt, having no one and having nothing to look forward to, lying here with so much broken, and to have cancer running, I don't think I have any more strength, and my tears are running out. For me to be heartless, without love being velvet, to this life, I'm so sick, wishing there was another way to live in It can't Stop Writing, My Hands Are Bleeding It shouldn't have to take me lose you, to show how you meant to me, always close, showing so much love, warming my heart, always pumping; I love you always. On my mind, there's nothing like the real thing; you can't find real until it's gone, Crying, writing to you, my love, one after another; Can't stop writing, my hands bleeding, blood barely moving, I can't stop: Every night, crying, writing... To you to read them, so much hurt. There were no goodbyes to our love. When I cry, I will try in love to lose you; my love, it hurts inside. The one I loved, even when I tried, love, it hurts without you. My love, I promised you'll always be my Maria, always my only treasure, my rare diamond. I don't want you to fade away without me. I am sorry I didn't protect you, my love; I can't sleep, as I'm always waking, always shaking, always getting sick, without your help keeping me together. My heart always hurts when there's a crack in my heart, I can't heal; so much pain in my head, spinning, drowning without you. My life with no feeling of being alone, never getting to hold you through these troubling times I have in My life, feeling broken, being without any warning, or dying almost of my heart. Won't let you go; There's no doubt about the fact I can't breathe, trying to be strong. Haven't seen you, my love, that we Always met in night, now I'm crying late, dying, so I have no body to call my love; I have so many Regrets that I never told you. I love you, my love. Can't be so lost without feeling so cold, every night feeling love gone, fading farther away from me; Love, this wasn't goodbye; so many scars, it's Taking me over with no closure. Unintentionally cared if you lived or die, for you to die, I'm sure my soul went with you that night we both went to sleep, waking up seeing, feeling I'm so cold. I'll never take advantage of life again.

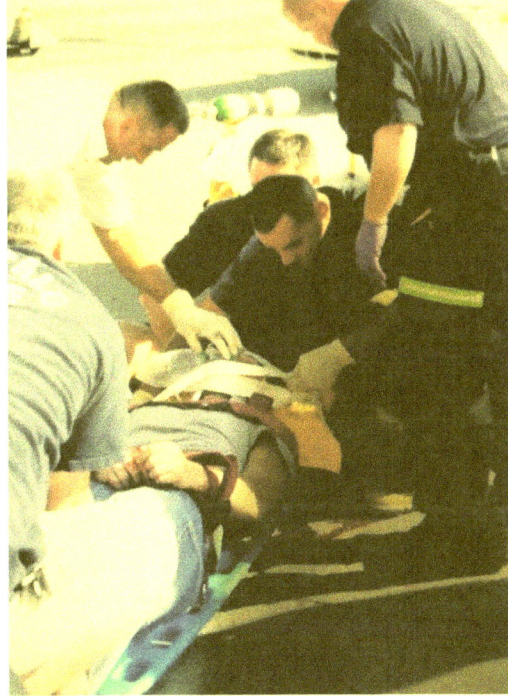

It took 15 years to learn don't take advantage of life, and love what to live for. Why I wasn't called in that day, to know I'm stronger; I'm here to help others, to be a leader in so many ways. Even if I crawl, I still get back up to be broken in those 30 years. To understand what life meant for much of my life with no end in pain, with cancer running, like that 18-wheeler struck me down. For my dreams to end at that time, thinking it was too late to say, "I'm sorry for taking advantage of life," then my love gone, just to have so much dust on my picture with her. My last feeling is to try to believe with this broken heart angel. The only light is to only find ways to try to live with this pain, wishing I could still hold her hand...

Without Her Here to Pull Me Back to Love

I don't deserve this; she was perfect, one and only love of my life, one and only dream. When I close my eyes at night, I'm hoping, lying in this empty bed, hoping to dream of my once love, so cold; looking down from the stars, are where... heaven called her. Now, my love Can't heal my broken heart, missing everything we had; Couldn't get over this dark reality I'm so scared of, I'm so without. I'm lying on this cold shower floor, stuck, knowing my world is ending. Young, without her to get me through it all hurts the most. I wish for her, remembering that I'll never get to hold her again, and I can't sleep without her here to pull me back to love....

My Love, I Don't Want to Run Away

I Promise You My love, I don't want to run away, I promise you, I will always love you. I need you here; Easy-to-use enough for you. My reason I give love to you, my friend, now, love, having so much, that we will never let go. We will feel so full in this world. When We get the chance to try to love each other, I know love isn't there any longer…

All My Sins Need Holy Water Without My

Used to being a bad bunny to one That's now cold, Wishing I could just kiss her hand one More time. Being a Romeo Losing his Juliet, A Romeo Now being so alone, thinking of her, to Never Finding love again. Being a bad bunny to now have no one to touch; being this snow bunny, now so cold, looking up to this moon That's always alone, looking for my Juliet. Being nothing but this Dying night, hoping for you, My Juliet, To Come home. Feeling a tear, roll on this cold cheek on this cold night, waiting, being alone, fading every day. Without your love, I'm dying slow. Just hear my heart; It's been missing Here Without You, my Juliet. I can't escape this pain of my love, that never got over you, That I can't love nobody, but you, my Juliet, No one Can Equal Our love. You, My Juliet, I miss you so much. Now Lost, You, My Juliet, even my Heart On this cold, dark Night. My true love, far out my Reach, to hurt Every time I look up, every breath I take, Hurts Without you. Thinking I was in love, to feel How it feels Here. Without my Juliet. I'm waiting alone, cold, being obsessed with love, being in addiction to hurt when all alone having nothing to hold through so many raining nights in the shower, hoping for love to fulfill my hurt. So many nights now cold, holding my pillows, looking for a woman who loves me for me without being just friends. I have so many of just wanting more, for the right one to come with a full heart, even when I try and fall to be getting back to find true love, even if it really hurts...

So Emotionally Scared Without Her

I'm so emotionally scarred and always up waiting For You To come home, Feeling so alone. My Love, to ease this pain, Because My mind is like a skating ring, just can't Get my mind right; Waiting for you, when you Were my... medicine, when I couldn't recuperate; every night, waiting for you to come back home to help Me, Fulfill My fantasy. That I'm So emotionally scarred, here without your love, it's phenomenal; It's driving me Crazy, Using the word love Is a duplicate, turning on this P.T.S.D., That's going over every One I fall with. To cry myself to sleep, wishing for help, at least a minute of peace in this life, I'm living With so much Phenomena of love, Crushing What I have Left with So much Depression. Every second that goes on, lying in this shower corner, crying over you, so emotionally scarred, wishing for hope to move on, When I'm starting to not love my self, every time I get close to love, to cry, To Predations That I can't never love Again, having tried, So many times. To be so emotionally scarred, knowing it can't be fixed, always over you, crying is the way I try, with so much hurt, needing you. Someone to help me; Please, save me, where are you when I truly need you? I Feel This Knife in my back When up alone, losing it, With The devil Playing games with our Love. My Anxiety, Always Being so sprung, Without You Love, Always Broken, I Can't Sleep Because I know you aren't safe from not coming home, where I'm always waiting Up For you to Show, Every night....

Can't Get Ahead

I'm sorry this is hard; the more I promise, the more give away my heart, I can't get ahead. In this life, I'm in seeing so many couples so happy me being alone with this pain, every holiday being so confused seeing so many… spending time; so many couples being so warm, happy; me being so cold, alone, and broken, always looking at the ground, with all shut outs on this edge I'm on, hoping for real love…

My Memories To Fade Away

Hello, My name is Greg, The Author And Writer Of these tragic memories of mine. The Times I have fallen in love to get hurt, always ending Alone, trying to get back up, but to always fall, I thank you for reading my many memories that always ends like a roller-coaster; I love you all, just know there's always Hope, and there is always someone out there for you…

Never Be Easley Replaced

I know it's not your fault; I don't know how to love. I know how much you taught Me about love and what it means, opening my mind; getting lost, my heart being so hypnotized, needing, Curling from your love, knowing you will Never be easily replaced with all the time we have left.

I'll always feel

My life Always on The Low End Of these Hurtful scars, That They will never go, so much, It hurts, So inside; My hands don't feel right, Writing to you. So much more, It Hurts The most because I know you can't answer. My heart is so cold, being so sorrowful, my love Now is watching. I'll never get to hold; I'll never get to grow; I'll always feel heartless. I'll always feel hopeless. I'll feel so gone, feeling so dark. On this path I'll always be on. Without you, my love...

I'm sorry, my angel

Please don't go, my love, stay one more night. I need you here; please don't say our love is fading farther. I hope our love isn't gone. My love, I know this isn't easy, living with your heart; I need you more than ever. I try to be with you; I hope our love is not gone. Every night, can't stop calling for you. Where are you, my love? I can't breathe without you. I'm so weak; I'm sorry. I need you here. Were you just not knowing? If I try every day to help me remind what love is, my wish is to come true, dear. My love, it's been forever; I'm holding my love; hope it isn't gone I'm sorry you're leaving my side, being a short time, I need you here with me. I know this isn't easy, knowing my love is gone…

My Heart Ripped

I can't love again. Without your love, without you, there are so many nights of many more tears. Without you, I'm so lonely. In this life going by without you, my only one, my all I deeply care about. To be without you, I'm broken, and no matter what I do reminds me of you, wishing I could have just had a little more; wishing for you in my life filled with so much hurt. I was in your life to end up without you for so many nights, now looking back at your pictures, feeling like I wasn't enough to you. Even though now we're far apart and my soul's so cold, so alone, having so much love for you, wishing I could have done more; every night, crying late to find out my true love is now my angel. It's not fear; there's no one to save me from this. Surrender life's pain, having no future, having my heart ripped out, missing my mamicita, wishing to be my Maria My heart with chains, no matter how much more pain I'm in, I will never change in the mirror, watching my love fly away. When I close my eyes, hoping to hold, hoping for my angel, my love that is so real, I'm so lost without her love...

All My Life It's Always a Struggle

Always seeing my mom Struggling Since I was young, watching, being helpless, trying to feed, but couldn't. No seed, not missing what I never had; being poor, walking these streets to learn how to survive this world Alone. Being all that I know; I'm not going to make it, being alone in these streets, as I feel I'll always be struggling…

Cold Fall Nights

This stress in my chest, in this dark fall night, not leaving my side. For my only one reason why I was hanging on to what's left of me, my heart being in the sand with no cure of water, so weak to make my heart on this. One thing I'm Sure of Is Love and Alone, finding somebody Who can I love...

You're Not Dreaming

As I lie here wishing I was in a dream where I know there's no pain for what I'm going through, Everyday being in this lonely, painful world that's a chain of pain; Every day with so much agony, Having cancer so young, watching My life gone with no love, Asking if there is anybody out there Because I'm still standing, Too. If they can help fall in love, feeling like no one. What's to know? I need to talk; my life is stuck on this cold floor, there are so many ways to get this written to the one who can help heal someone because I care more than myself...

Shattered in This Light

My life seems to be around rain, But I will not quit; My life is of darkness, With no light, With so much courage, But Feeling like this is my end, When I Can't see my focus, Always Feeling twisted, Even When I can't breathe, Always Trying to not give in. With having nothing to fall back on and having nothing to fall forward with,

Just to fall to my knees, Praying, to ask why I just keep losing, always to cry and write to whomever would listen. To my representing and my Unfulfilled potential In This lonely world, I'll Always Be Hurting, but am always Trying, To Try to live My life With So much agony of missed dreams; With This broken heart That shattered... In this light, I cry at...

Out of Chains

I'm running out of reasons for you to be holding my heart on these chains. That hurts, being alone; Without you, I have so many scars. Starting to show, outside being so cold, I can't pretend I don't keep looking up because I had a lot to lose. My heart being so chained to you, I need you to my break these chains, to survive without you, where my life, I Can't Deny, I'm Chained To you, My Heart Not Letting Go. I Can't lie here without you; my life isn't right. I'm losing here without you; my life is fading farther from my perspective than you can imagine. How I'm losing my mind because you never see My life with no luck without you; My life with no end in this life alone; My life without my heart and won't be another…

Burning Up Solo

I wasn't selfish enough to bring you closer to me. For my first time, I was to be a loner, keeping it low, walking with this fake smile, burning up endlessly. My love, having so much loved to do this on my own, burning up solo is the only light; I have no velvet to love. So little; ALWAYS So lost in this Internal silence, Missing How you Lie Here with me. Meanwhile, you are my shadow, close to my heart That Won't be able to go. Even though I know you are far but close Here in my heart, Alone on This New Year's Eve night Where I'm Losing my mind, how you broke me. Now I'm so alone, having this pain In My heart that Won't let you go, where There's no lie, my lover; My life just beginning Without you Here beside me Where I sit, outside your house alone on this cold night, feeling so Sorry to My once Loved one That's gone. I'll always love And I'll always come back, Even If she's far From my touch, She'll always be in my heart...

Time I wish I had more of

I just need more time in this life to make a difference and time to grow with these emotions, having no fairy tale to my life, having no more feelings to say I had love to end, with my dream, with no endless hurt, being broken, better, with my heart bleeding. Without you, love, impossible to come home to see you're not here; you're gone, wishing I could be there for you. My heart hurt the most we went our separate ways. I go without; my head hurts with this. Impossible without you, crying late, wishing it wasn't real; crying late, wishing I was with you; coming to nothing but memories, wishing I had more time for you to show my love. Feeling I'm in prison without your help, having nowhere to sleep; up for days having this addiction of what I have for you, my once love. To be wishing I wasn't lonely, broken hearted, wishing I had more time with you; having no time to fall, in love with you, to feel it when you're gone...

Not even close

I was almost there; not knowing why every time I got ahead to not, as it wasn't my fault. God gave me a chance to be a good man through this life where it's hard to trust my life with these broken hearts. I feel like putting it on paper so people can hear me and the shit I'm in going with, so much drain with all of my love. To be alone, it hurts without her tearing me apart, a part of me with it, not getting better, going to sleep, angry, crying for above, and hardly breathing. I beg it's hurting trying to always try to fall in this heart- beat racing, drowning on my knees, crying, having no time to make me cry as I am by myself; having no shadow following me. I have learned that I never get off this cancer ride, so twisted a roller coaster, I can't get off, always looking at my end, every night crying for above for taking everything I knew, and with being so blue, my mind becomes more silent with life going wrong, not feeling what it is but just pain; heartache with so much hurt, not having true love, for it to be without. Just get dirt thrown at me with no love to love me. I'm up waiting for this pain to stop being full, at times, wanting to cry, walking with a fake smile, always stuck at this red light alone, coming from having no one to help grow with being on top, to lose, to know what I had to feel: Hopelessness to keep saying this pain I'm in, to know this is real, with the sand going to stop, an I'm alone. Did I fail at finding real love? I'm hoping to run to someone. That could be lying to me; if there's real love, feeling everyone is gone...

What Is Left of My Love

What is left of my love is going to die,

With me; There was no taking of what I Learned, Struggling Always to Take One Step, to fall back; Having no buddy to catch Me, it hurts to struggle to make it, to fall on my knees, crying, Having so much heat. To have so much Go wrong young, having cancer Young, to getting hit by a semi and to have a so much, to end with nothing. To help get back up, it's going to take more for the devil to take this soul. I'm having so many angels to pretend to wipe these tears away, to struggle with so many pieces of my heart, that're gone with so many Loves To die with them while I lie there alone, having no one. Once had it all, to be Now fading...

My Love, Where Are You?

How can you love? when I'm so scared for you, giving someone your heart to get it taken, and scared little by little, every second without them, what started out a fantasy is becoming reality in this dark, deep; Inside this broken angel, without my dream feeling so real, still alone, fading farther, hoping to see her again. To have, not only to hurt; what started a small scar but to have so many starting to show through, bleeding hurt, love going on without them. Lost without, broken, can't hold on; letting go with so many pieces gone that can't be fixed....

My Fractured Heart

My mind is so fractured, my heart that's so much broken, in so many moonlights, my love that always comes, attending as a star shining bright, Like your Smile once more. In my life, without you, it gets so cold, with this dark shadow Closing in on me, with no more goodbyes, having a tragic life that spilled us in this dark night where I can't stop loving you; my only friend, gone, making my life harder, thinking of you, every night crying for the above for taking us apart. Now I'm walking alone, having nothing to hold, through so many raining days like this, isn't life not meeting you again in this dark fall Night, where there was no time for us anymore? Every day that goes without you in my life, always feeling So dark, Falling, so hard, losing you, the one I Love the most with my Shattering heart, missing all what we had, MY LOVE...

My Love

Love, when we are together, it feels like heaven on Earth when we walk together. Love, you bring more to my life going Under, having to be close to my heart on my Knees, begging to you, if I can hold you Through the nights, even for the rest of our Lives, being glad I found the girl of my Dreams, being stronger than anybody. For so many nights, kissing me slow, and inside my arms, I'll never let go. I wish I could go back in time to grow together; I would love her longer in this life. My love, I always I can't stop loving, my heart will always be full....

Future of Darkness

My future seems to be nothing but darkness; my life with no feeling of love, I'm not even ready to let go. This last piece of my life is gone. Every night, can't stop Me from crying; My heart never got to love again When she will not say something. Every night, I was crying late, hoping to hear her, but to hear nothing at all but my weeping. Not having her, my heart, my world, That I can't give up. My love, that always makes me feel real....

My Beloved

My sweet friend, when I look in to your I see my beloved. Looking back. I am no end, up with a broken hollow chest, I need help with this bleeding heart, thinking of her, losing her, holding you; I can't get over her, holding on Until I pass away from my beloved having so much pain, being in denial Everybody looks like her; Everybody smells like my beloved with her perfume that's driving me to drink more. I'm not sure how, too, When I cry, when I keep seeing my beloved smiling back, I can't fix it. So, I don't hurt, but I keep running out of reasons why I can't get my beloved out of my head when I was so much in love ..

Please Take Back This Pain

All I want more is for my once love to knock once more on this cold door. All I want is to see my once love once again. All I want is peace in this life, having so much pain, with this cancer in my Blood, with this Broken heart and All I want Is to be loved once more Before it's too late. All I want is to stop hurting inside, having no one to fix my scars from bleeding. All I want is my heart to stop dying for love because I hurt for so many nights, crying of this pain I'm in, being broken, a shattering angel with his wings broken off. All I want is to not be lonely anymore. All I want is my life. Without this cancer, in my blood, my love to come back to me, so when it's time, I go Peacefully with No more hurting…

My Darkness Turning to Dust

Now, Far, so cold, holding on to my nights, always giving Time to women, to end, Starting to Feel This pain, being alone, having no one To listen to me, but just let it go. At night, crying for above for my sympathy, fading in this dark, cold night, thinking of so many warm nights, Having Now No more. Being hard to move on, I am always thinking of once. My life now without you, It's My Darkness, Turning to dust. My heart always hurts, dying slow inside...

A Broken New Year's Eve

I'm falling in, so apart, my heart is barely, I'm so scared of this life, I'm so lonely and broken on this New Year's Eve night, being so Used to holding your love That's Now gone, seeking answers, crying, Late to Wishing It Was me, not you, my once loved, THIS wasn't was supposed to be. Hoping this was going be pure, being so Rare, Love, I have fallen for, So I Hurt More When I don't have you. When I told you I'll never, But I Don't have no one To save me from So Much Hurt on this New Year's Eve. My life with no end, with so much hurt, lost inside, here, without you, here on this dark, cold night, wishing I could go back to get my love before it ended short ...

Can't Feel a thing

Every day's breaking me so much, I just can't feel anything anymore. Love, I gave it my all to feel like a Viking killing myself with a broken heart, scared of this life. I'm so sick; there was a crime I did not know about my life, not so much, but high anxiety about the fact that there will never be another; she was my all in a short period of my life. My life without her, not being able, and I know this takes a lot to get this darkness to just live with so much pain to be lonely with no cure for her to come back, but now be a broken heart without true love again...

Set Me Free

I ASK THE LORD, PLEASE SET ME FREE FROM THIS SURRENDERED LIFE. To begin life Without her here, I'm losing it; I can't survive without her. I used to have a heart on this sleeve; Now Can't find my heart. It died with her. My heart is so sorrowful, so much hurt, so much sacrificing to hurt, feeling like I'm the one dying slowly in the morgue with her. My only, my favorite girl I'd picture Close by my Heart That I never told her she was my only one. My First love of all my dreams, now I didn't think I'd Know how to love again when I gave her My love, every night, waiting by my window to hold her, cuddle the night way. I'm not used to being alone, never getting to hold her.

My LUV hurts

My luv, I don't know about you, but I hope loving you isn't a crime because I have fallen for you. My luv, the first time I saw you, I could see I was falling deep inside, close to my heart, waiting for someone like you for a long time. Please let me love you; I've never fallen in love. You are the one; I just want to try to be with you. My luv, I'm in love with you, you driving me loco. I want you; I've fallen in love. You are my true angel, let me love you....

My Bleeding Love

My bleeding heart, dying slow from so many scars, my life can't catch a break; My love is gone, my heart, I can't find. I'll never get to give it another try. My nights are cold lying here on this floor, my hope fading farther from me. My whole life is gone; I'm feeling so alone. My days round, and round Up and Down Drowning without warning. My hour glass, Running from me; My scares won't heal, My soul on chains. Mysterious, my secret, my lover, my friend with lust Is gone....

My Little Secret

This is undeniable, a little secret; I feel so bad. When she turned, it was the last I saw my little secret. When she came to me, I turned; she went to jail. She passed away; now I have to live with turning on her when she needed me the most, the last I will see of my little secret No one in my heart I never got to say "I love you"; she came over night, started in lust to making love, just never getting say it to my little secret. I feel so alone in this world we live. In a short time, she was the only person who was in your arms. My life's been a long time without her here for me to tell her I'm sorry for turning on her when she needed me the most; I can go on without having what I have done every time, I close my eyes. Please, can I have one more chance to save her? Knowing she was in such a panic and in so much pain only to find the doctors telling me there's nothing they could do to save her, she's in no more pain. It all went to my heart, hurting, feeling scars that will never heal. I never said... my last goodbye to my always little secret. I should have never when she needed me.

My Love Keeps Running in My Mind

I can't get you out of my head, my love, there's some kind of addiction I have for you; I just can't get over you. I'm lying dying here. Without your life, I can't pretend; can't stop loving you, my life feeling broken, being without your love when we were so close, living this life, What I am to do without your love? It's an addiction, so lost without your lust. I'm broken, my heart can't be fixed. Crying is how I can justify this love. My dear friend, my lost love, it kills me to say I still care for you, and all I can do is let my heart bleed. I'm hurt, being so sick, having your love gone, making me cry. Why I can't breathe? Drowning without you, I'm feeling so alone, empty without saying my last goodbyes you. My love, I can't get you out of my head; so many scars that hurt; it's hard to say "I love you," My life has so much hurt. Why? One more for God's bidding, I promised I'll always have You; now so lost without your life ending, young, being a broken angel. I need you here to wipe these tears away. Just don't want you to see me like this, so hurt, crying, late, hoping to hold you for one more cold night; I pray for you, my love ....

I Hoped More of

I hope my life will never end; it's just starting. I still never found my true love. I hope my life will never end short without love. I still never got married; I hope to before it's too late. even if it's for a second in this life. I am living, hoping there's more to life than this. I'm in trying to be strong, holding me back, keeping me on a chain, knowing I can't breathe, trying to live for a true love I can hold through the nights we have left…

I Can't sleep

Dear my love, It's 3:00 in the morning; I just can't sleep without you here, my love. Where are you? Dear my love, it's 3:45 now, my love, you're not answering my calls. There are so many thoughts go on in my head, spinning, drowning without you, I'm feeling, so surrender to my heart that's never-ending. Dear my love, it's now 4:56; I have just got a phone call. I just lost you, but not your love. Dear my love, it's 6:00 in the morning writing my last text. I got a call; you're never coming back. I'm in love with you. There's no one else I wanted to with more than you. I just can't get over you; nobody made me feel the way you did, love. I always see you in my dreams...

I Gave My All

My love, my all, my love, I promise you I'll love you and life and more. My love, I promise you are not in no more pain. I will take you in, put you in this heart, I promise you, your love will linger me always. My love, Promise I will look to Sky, waiting for you. Now your star is getting harder, farther Than I want… I find a way for us to get together. Without my love Having gone, I promise I will always love… I just need you Here where I'll always love having you in my arms. My love's disappearing, so much velvet love, so little life, so much hurt….

Please Don't go

Don't go, not now; we had so much passion for each other for you to go. Don't go, not now; I'm such a broken angel, being so sick, sitting here alone. Don't go, not now; My heart is going to be empty, hurting, getting our lives ripped in two, now being lonely. Don't go, not now; I can't feel nothing. It's turning numb, lying in this dark shadow close to my heart, and never can get to heal. Don't go, not now. My love that is disappearing, when I wake, you start to fade away, To the next night where There's no light in the dark, fall night, waiting to see her again. Now so lost, I'm fading without her until my next dream...

Your Love Has Me Melting

Your love has me melting; I need an intervention from your lust, broken my heart, never healing. Your love is a chain; that is the only one who I need to be with, the one only with bleeding love. I can't stop calling my love, having so much to give. My heart Won't let you get away. My love, it's going to be okay. I will never change when I'm in love with you changed my life, without you, I'm by My side, my mind turning Every second. I breathe. I take without you, love, having gone far without me. My love, I'll never shut you out, Love, having gone always feel your halo… You are my true angel of mine, always shining Bright, lighting my life. It's way too long, I love you, my love. Can't be so independent, so much hurt, no more spark; Without you, my heart won't let go or be another one. I loved her; to end without her crying or dying, with me fading in this world, we are just not meant to be holding her, kissing her, or being in love. Once to be baby, I was to be with you. Baby, I'm in love; you're … driving me crazy. You're all I think about. You're my life; you just don't know what you are doing to me. Without you love, I'm falling apart....

How Much Time Wasted

How much wasted time? I have to face the fact your love is gone; if I tell you I'm sorry, I don't think it would matter. I have to face the fact I'll never see your smile; I've been running from my demonstration; losing you made me a half a man, not loving myself, a sinking boat with its captain. I've got to face the fact that your love's not coming back. Knowing you are my all, I'm lost, broken on this cold floor, praying for you, my love. I can't face the fact I can't live without your love; we were so much more. You were my reason for why I was more than a half, I was whole with you in my life. Now feeling broke, I can't stop loving you; all I wish is that I could have been there more. Without you, I'm just half a man. I have to face the fact, your love...

is gone. If I tell you I'm sorry, I don't think it would matter. I face the fact I'll never see your smile; I'm running from my demonstration. Losing you made me a half man, not loving myself, a sinking boat with its captain. I've got to face the fact that your love's not coming back. Knowing you are my all, I'm lost, broken on this cold floor, praying for you, my love. I can't face the fact that I can't live without your love. We were so much more; you were my reason for why I was more than half; I was whole with you in my life. Now feeling broke, I can't stop loving you. I wish I could have been there more. Without you, I'm just half a man....

Grow Old With You, Love

My love, I want to grow old with you; my love, knowing what it means to have you, I want to grow old with you. You have so much love, looking into your eyes, hoping to grow old. The more we grow, the more our love .... strengthens. You are my true love with velvet love; I always will cherish your million kisses. What we have is velvet; in this life, our love is so strong. My love, I want to grow old with you, waking up with you, having so much love, so strong, too weak, broken apart. Tearing me from your lust broken dream, I can't hear or touch my love having gone....

When does my morning end

When does my morning end for life to begin without my love the one love of my once loved heart never healing right without my love. When does my morning end for life to begin drowning without nobody to help wishing there was no pain for love to end no one calling without my love. When does my morning end for life to begin without my best friend my love is so lost without feeling so empty weak turning blue she was my end to my beginning I'm drowning without her here, to be alone having just a ending asking myself when does it stop, and when does my morning end for life to begin to just see her in dreams that brings memories of my love to fall in nights hoping holding of the rest i have of my love crying holding my pillows tight....

The More I Miss You

The more I hurt, the more I cry, The days go without having you there, less you're by my side, I call your phone, and it just rings, driving me to cry. The question is how being so young, not thinking of love, just like a nightmare, Wishing I was just letting her go, but she struck in Dark, my head spinning, drowning in this love wasn't enough to bring me up without her tearing me awake. Then I cried without her.

It only took one heartbreak, to be made single, less love; without her, days are going dark, just like a nightmare, wishing I was just in her arms.

My heart is barely moving, starting to stiffen like I'm beginning to fade away, and I'm too bad at goodbyes. love. The more I hurt, the more my heart breaks, the more I cry without my love. Leaving here in this life alone, Having nothing but pics from me, an angel of mine. The more I hurt, less of my once-love taken from these beautiful skies, looking For a woman who loves me more is not an angel of God....

My Angel, My Lost

Why my love, my best friend; Why my love, my best friend, I'm wishing to see every moment of this story to end short, Being so blind for her only to be taken. Why, my love, my love, I can't get over him, lying, dying with my pride letting me cry. Why did it have to my best friend, my love? Why my love, my friend, I'm so broken angel without my lover; My life just beginning to end. It's just starting to fall. Without my love, without my best friend, I promised I always have in my heart, never heal my mind; I never forget. My love, my friend, my angel, seeing your halo,

I know you were always by my side, forever night I watch for you,

My love, my angel, my friend....

A Peasant

Life is like a peasant, life like a peasant having no father, seeing my mama work so much. It hurts for so many days. Life is like a peasant just to live a life to get pushed back when trying to get back up; life like a peasant is hard, stress getting looked at differently ....

My All

She is so beautiful, she gags me when seeing her. She's not hurting anymore, just I am. She was first, and it hurts to have her be my last, And I can't love nobody back but her. She was my reason why I tried love, and I can't try it without her by my side to help me heal, to numb this pain away from this broken heart wishing for hope.....

I Need Someone

I'm lying broken on this floor, praying, asking for more, crying, I need someone who could be my Hero, so broken angel, I'm so alone Here I lie on my floor in this dark place; it's no longer love I feel It's hurt and the pain, feeling alone in this dark place, feeling her memory drift further and further Away as my heart tries to heal, longing for her touch and missing her, Feels like she's fading away further and further from my heart and My love To a special someone, I lie on this cold floor, praying for the first love of all my memories going To die without her, Tearing me; So many scars, So dark sky, alone, waiting for her, Even when I try, every night crying late, hoping I was just dreaming and already missing her. Why can't I hold on with no end? I'd rather run but have no feelings in my legs, feeling stiff, like I'm next to you. My love, It can't be, So lost; So much hurt; So broken. It can't be true; where are you, my love? Can't be. So many raining nights, hoping to see you in my life, only to hurting trying to hide in this dark life. Going on fire, so lost badly without your love....

I Don't Want to Be Left Alone

I can't lie; my life has been hard, losing you, knowing I love you. In this life with no wings, I know you're my angel. My heart feels you wipe my tears away. I'm never letting you go. There's isn't no pleasant thing; losing you, I don't want to be alone. Without you, my love I have for you can't go away from me because of how strong our love was. ....

Missing You

I miss you and all that we had; I miss you and all that we had… Oh, how it hurts without you, how it broke me so much, not having you. I Can't pretend that what we had wasn't real. I still hear your voice in this dark night, crying for you, holding on to my pillows. Not having you holding me, it's driving me to cry. When I look in this beautiful sky, looking for your star, hoping to get a hold of you, my love, and having so much broken, it can't be real. Without your love Having my heart, feeling so lost without You in my life. I'm alone, raining every day without you, my love, I can't wait to see you again having tried so many nights now cold, Not holding you in this dark life, I'm not sure how to love again without you, love, heaving My heart filled with hurt feeling, so without you, my life is on its own way to hurt without you. My love, I miss what we had more than before God's bidding, watching my scars grow without you….

Dear Mother

My mother, I found a love, not knowing what it was to until her ending this world. Mother, I found a love so sweet, I can't stop holding her to my heart. Mother, I found a love she pretty, so bright, lighting my life; she's so perfect. Mother, I have a love; she's my angel, my everything; My love having gone far without me only hurts, hit by Loneliness, can't sleep; I've been up to broken with no love, wishing I could have woken her up. Mother, I have found a love gone, fading farther than I thought; I need I never let her go, feeling like I let her out, my love having to go to I am by myself. Please, help, without my love, her life just staring, seeing me in my eyes, hoping to hold her in this cold night. Without my love; where are you? I say every night that I never get be with my love, watching me above…

I'll Never Let Go

I told you I never let go, but I lost you and my heart, In the same night, crying late to find true love lying here hurts more. I gave you, my heart. My life with no water; so weak, turning to the fact I can't stop. Loving you isn't a crime because I have fallen in love, now realizing that You are my angel; my life not so far without you, my love. Can't sleep well; you're gone. It's tossing, turning, looking, cold; holding nothing, for you were my pillow, late through so much pain, being a shoulder to cry on. For me to be alone, just so in love with you, there's isn't no more tears; I'm lonely, broken; lost myself in this shattered mirror, watching my soul go away from me...

It really hurts

I really don't like to talk about this; it really hurts. I really don't like to talk about my life; it really hurts every day. I am sitting in this dark corner, trying to fight back. It just keeps falling in pain. My life is on its second term with so much going wrong. My life is nothing but hurt, being on a ventilator, trying to breathe. It just hurts trying to gasp for air, having so much broken. My heart is trying to fix, knowing that I can't. My life, always hurting, trying to hide it in this dark life, having so much that needs fixing, starting to feel alone. I can't leave this corner, shaking, asking for forgiveness, for my life is just going under, having nothing but health issues; broken love, knowing that it can't be fixed; Knowing so much is broken, it can't be fixed "Crying is the way to go. I'm always alone; a fight every day to live longer, I'm trying to find real love, I hope it won't be cut short in this life, I had so many fears before falling asleep every night.

I am not Feeling this Life I just want to hold someone. I have nobody else; I can't find my way through this life that is spilled apart from the rest of love that I left, having no end in pain, not finding love. My Heart will never Believe in True Love Again, just to have no love...

My Once Beloved

I still think of your true heart moments. I still think of the nights we had, even the cold nights. I still think of you, my perfect angel, every time I close my eyes, I hope to see you in my dreams at least one more time. I still think of you, my love; you are my first love; you were my all. I still think of the night of losing you, my love; I couldn't stop holding my pillows, hoping I get to hold you again. It's driving me crazy; I can't stop thinking you. We have so much in my first love. I still think of her, all the nights she stayed, now she gone and it's tossing, turning, looking nobody holding; now lonely. I still think of her. I let her go; Tears just keep following; feet getting wet, still thinking how the sky never gets lonely. I still think of the love I once had, how I can't live without her up there. I'm losing it, on my knee; I don't know why she was taken from me. Only the Lord knows, I just wish I could see my love again....

Being so cold

My heart is so cold in a cold box, my love is so now broken. My soul is on chains, My life feels like I am a puppy dog in a dog pound, waiting for a home, behind bars. My pain from the loss of her; My health is going belly-up, having so much going wrong. My voice whispered from being so speechless of missing her; my mind turning every second of my life like a clock. I'm looking for peace of mind,

My knowing that this takes time to heal…

My wish is gone when my love died….

I'll wait to see my love

I'm standing outside, feeling cold air hit my face while I look in this dark night, crying for her to come and save me. I'm not in a safe place without her tearing me apart; my love is gone, making me sad without my heart. My days round up without her; I'm on bumping grounds that I'll never be able to hold her. I felt love being in denial about her life, just staring; Seeing her reflection, feeling that her end of this life, I'm so much hurt, so much broken, love, having to do Days of my life without her, Days are just longer…

My Heart Chained

My heart with chains that will never break; my heart never healing with my life on its way. Without her, there's so much more hurt, missing her, knowing I'm giving up without her. Days are burning up endlessly; my heart is on fire, so hurt, so much inside every day that goes by, wishing... I was in her arms, now holding this pillow late, crying with my chained heart that won't let her go, begging for her to come back, to break these chains that hold me or stood behind me for who I am...

My Velvet Love Gone

So much velvet love, so little life, so much hurt, so lost without her; it's internal silence. So much velvet of love having gone in nights, hoping, trying, being, but keep falling, hitting the ground, crying late, hoping to love before I die. Without my love having gone far without me, to only cry with little velvet love, a sorrowful soul; I'm wishing there was another way of life without my love…

Wishing It Wasn't Her

You're my only, my love; I love nobody but you. Every night, I go watch the morgue, wishing it wasn't real, crying late to wishing it wasn't true. I lost you, lost within. I wish I could escape this dream; without you, love, we were so strong together; weak broken apart tearing me up from your heart that isn't easy, living by myself in this dark shadow close to my heart, never believing. My love, the moonlight is the only light I have to find you in this dark, fall night. Where are you now? So lost without my love; your heart won't die. I need you here. What am I supposed to do? Days are getting harder, thinking of you once; my love, vice versa, is here waking up to a broken heart, wishing I was just letting you know I love you. My dear friend, my love is going far. Without you by my side, in my arms tonight, I will always close my heart. There's no pretending; just strong love for you. Where are you, my love? I can't live without you, feeling so empty; colder every night. Feeling love wasn't enough to bring you back to life, going on fire, so lost, so dark inside with you to be without. I wish I could go back, knowing how lucky I was to have you, wishing I could hold you until your life ended, young having no love to save me from this. Surrender life; begin drowning without you, feeling so surrendered to your life going by without you, my love Can't be true.

Isn't No Road Like What We're On

There isn't no road like it, falling in love, wishing I can make you rich in love, holding you. There isn't no road like broken inside when you lose your true love. There isn't no road like feeling so alone, not having love; You give me strength, losing my mind, lying to myself to be without you. There's isn't no road like this one I'm on without you, love, feeling so poor in this cold basement. Started out young, having no love, having a chance of life, my love having gone, crying, writing to my heart, never healing. Your love is so strong; without my love beside me, so alone; I just want to be alone, just so in love with you. There's isn't no road like this one, having nothing to hold After your life ended young, being short, just hope you can see me Dying slow inside, the one I'm having so much brokenness of heart for. There's isn't no road like this one, my angel. Where are you now? So lost without your life, not knowing if I was just dreaming, about to wake you from my love. I can't breathe; Drowning without You, my love. Can't Be true, love hurts, I'm lying here, wishing I was in your arms. My heart is cold; My mind turns blue; There's isn't no road like this one. My eyes are not ready to open up without you. Where are you, my love? There's isn't no road like this one. Can't be true; I can't get over you. I'm lying, dying slowly in mysterious ways that I never told you I love you so, broken angel.

There's isn't no road like this one. I'm so lonely; please, help me survive this dark shadow close to my heart. I won't let you go. There's isn't no road like this one; I have nobody that loved me like you did, wishing you'd come back home. I have nobody to call love. I'm Mr. Lonely; trying to find you, my true love, I have nobody to save me. I need you here. I never told you that

I love you; I need you back to tell you how I feel about you. There's isn't no road like this one, needing you to be with me, feeling I never told you that I love you, deeply feeling so alone on raining nights, just hoping I see you again. To be without you, love, having gone to a better place, I've forever lost my love; forever lost my friend. There isn't no road like this one until we meet again. I'll be there for you, my love, still wishing I can hold you at night, my love. There's isn't no road like this one, angel. Where are you, love? I will never surrender in this life without you....

So Rare, So Pure

So rare, so pure; Our love is. Our love so pure, having so much energy in this life, shining bright like lightning. Our love so pure, not knowing what it feels to have rainy days; Always sunny, always warm, our hearts always pumping. Our love so pure, doesn't matter, With or Who, Rich, or poor, you couldn't buy it. I love how it's so real and can't put a price on it; It's so priceless. You just hope it never slips away. My love feels like velvet...

It's Cold With No Love

My love, know I always love you, My love, I know you own my heart, My love, know even though you're above watching, I have to move to find love, so I can hold through the Nights being so cold, My love, it's hard to give someone else the rest of my love, To fall in love again when I gave you Most of my heart, My love, I always look to your star every night going on Until we get hold each other once more. I'm sorry I ignored My love, I'm sorry I saw and did nothing but ignore; it was time I'd chosen to close my eyes, not knowing it was the least time I was going to see you. And it hurts with this pain, having to be close to love, to lose you, my all; deeply feeling, so hurt, I turned my back on my secret love. I never got tell her told how much she was so much loved by me, and I wish I never had turned on her the last time I saw my little secret...

My life got stiff

She was my all. When she ended it, my heart started breaking. She was my end to my beginning, starting to stiffen like I'm in the morgue with her. You going on without your love, having so much love, wishing she'd come back to your home, so Broken, your life not living in this shattered life, going on fire; So, lost, So damn cold. Crying, she left me here alone...

Oh, it hurts more. I let her in for my heart to bleed more; She never told me goodbye.

I feel I Can't stop. She was my end of my love, to fall in nights when she was my end, too. My heart won't let her go, wishing I could never let her go. Without her holding on, my heart won't fill without her tearing me wake from my love that I never told her how I felt, wishing I could have just have told her that I was in love, now realizing that she wasn't coming to my rescue, crying late, hoping to see her being broken, shattering every night, crying for her to come back to fix and knowing lucky I was to have her, now lost. I miss how much I had with her. I'm running out of reasons why she broke me. First love, now gone far without her to only hurts, hit by loneliest; can't wait for her, the only one I give all my heart, my love. Just can't get over reality; can't live without you, my love. Can't be so many memories going out; I feel, nemesis, it's not ready for her to end. No one calling, my love having so much broken, it can't be fixed. Crying, you left me alone. I can't speak; can't breathe; can't escape. My love ended; can't move, starting to stiff up without my love....

My Life in a Nightmare

There was a time I never felt pain.

There was a time in my life when I was unstoppable, playing football, an 18-wheeler struck me down and ended all my dreams. There's a time when I'm on my third life, just trying to find my way out of this hell, there was a time in my life when I finally found love for it to end so short, in a tragic way; so much pain that I'll always have so deeply inside. There's a time in my life, Feeling broken, being without anybody, feeling that I'm not a somebody; Now there's a time in my life Where I'm tired of being in this nightmare I'm in, Asking for strength to fight off this cancer that's running in my veins, Feeling unlucky, And no one can save me ,

In this nightmare I'm living in.....

I'm dying slowly without you

I'm dying slow and have no one to save me.

I'm dying slow, and I'm killing myself with broken love, having so many scars starting to show. I'm dying slow, and it's killing me. My once big heart now can't find my own, not having love, being my loneliest I have ever been. I'm dying slow, and it's killing me. Always, every night, being alone, being hurt, that's all I have.

Every time I fell asleep, when she left my side,

I was in denial, as she was my Boo, and now she is gone. Far away that I couldn't ever imagine...

So Many Bitter Nights

My nights are cold; without my love, it's Tossing, turning, being cold in my bed, having nobody next to me. My nights are cold with chills going down my spine, For so many nights, I'm feeling like I'm in a nightmare. I wish she could say something; I'm trying not to give up on once I loved, wishing my once my love to Please, say... something. My nights are cold; I'm still so codon where you were next to me, where we once held. It's not the same; it's so cold; I wish I could still be with you one more night to say how much love isn't the same without you....

I cannot pretend

I can't pretend; I am no thief for this Lord to take without having no love to fall apart from her life going by without me. Fading, my days are longer, having a half heart on fire, so I lost so badly without the way. I'm just not beating my heart, won't be the same; there isn't nothing but raining days, like this isn't real, crying for my soul to end it all, deeply feeling like I can't breathe, drowning in my tears that roll down this broke soul to be gone, for the ones I'm having this dark, fall night, crying late, dying slowly in this life, alone, having nothing but hurt. No more spark. Without knowing that this is a dream, I can't hear, touch my heart on fire; so lost, so dark inside within my heart on this cold, dark, fall night, crying late, wishing it would stop hurting me, for the way my life is on a deep end, wishing for you now, I'm so lost without your lust, broken dreams. My love having gone, crying is not my fault God took her so young, watching me cry; why I can't move, cold heart to be alone, having just been crucified and wishing I had someone to save me. To be heartless without my life, it's way too much more hurt, so I'm asking for someone to save me from so much hurt, so many scars, so much bleeding love Can't get over you; I'm lying, dying slowly in this life with your love is gone. If I tell you I'm sorry; I'm tired; I've had so much broken loss. I can't understand it. Why is falling in love making me sad without my love having gone? Crying, writing to my love, there will never be another; you are the reason why I tried love....

True Love Hurts

True love is hard find, walking miles with no beauty inside, trying to hide your smiling star once looking alone, having nothing but these troubles in my heart , True love hurts, even short in your life, Not knowing if it was with the one who you give your Love to end short, being So young, So blind, now broken in tears when I say I loved her to end short. True love lying here, waking; can't sleep, feeling like I need rehab for love having gone crying, writing all night, shaking, feeling so cold every moment, feeling like I'll never heal right Without a love, I just keep trying to be strong, but heaven keeps calling. True love having gone to a place to stay in this dark corner closing to my beginning, starting on a new life without love, falling to my knees, Begging God just to be with the true girl, the one Love. Without my love, her life just starts to hurt. How much love means to hurt, even if you can't see, there's so much hurt, so many scars; So dark inside without my love…

I Want You to Know

I know you'll always be close by, but not so far, knowing you live in my heart where you'll always be. I know you'll always wipe my tears away sadly, nor you can find me meaningfully with my heart Broken, just not beating, just like love gone. I know you'll be my angel to protect me, but it just hurts; I never want to see you go. My life's just so much hurt, so many nights. I know you'll be out of my life, but not my heart won't let you. You are my love of my life with no end ….

Never Knew What Love Was Until It Was Gone

Never knew what love was until she died, falling to my knees, knowing she was my last to fall in love; now I'm not doing alright. My love's disappearing, for me to hurt inside, losing her, for me just learning what love was. So much... pain I never felt before; God's bidding, I was just trying to love, and not knowing it was so painful to be loved, and losing love how it hurts more inside. When She isn't with me; I'm So lonely. Please just let me love you; I already gave You my heart, my soul, what else do I need to do to be with you? Why did you have to go? I just started to love; I can't go on trying, not without a love …

Nobody

When I keep going to sleep, waking up and seeing I'm alone, having no one in these arms, my life's feels so harder being used to love and leaving me without any warning, not before I give them something that can't be replaced. When the last time I gave someone my all, so deeply loved, the Lord taking, the time to make me a spell that I couldn't resist having her holding me, and keeping her always closer ....

Fading Away

Now life is fading away from a love that is gone to a batter place without me. As are Memory being all; I wish more of love from my Mamacita to be my Maria. as I'm so lost without her lust, my broken life, never meeting Her in this dark fall, in love, not knowing If I was to be without Her love having gone far to help me through these troubling times, I'm now So lost without, feeling so empty, weak, turning blue; my heart is cold, holding my pillows, crying late to her; my love It can't be true I can't live without you, and I hope we meet somewhere down the line...

I Need Love

I need love; it's getting harder to breathe without love. Please, come save me. I need love to make me feel I'm enough and feel a kiss on my lips once more. I need love. As I'm so lonely, broken hearted, wishing I had a heart on this sleeve.

I need love. Feeling like never getting over to find true love hurts, lying here, waking without my true angel, without my girl of dreams. I need love. I have no one to call my own life going by without her here, without a love; Every day, it's been so much hurt. I need love. So many nights crying, wishing some way to find true love; It hurts lying here, waking, drowning without finding true love hurts, lying to be alone…

In This Fall Night

I'm sitting here in this dark, fall night. Where are you now? Your star is getting farther. I'm sitting here in this dark, fall night; I wait, looking in this beautiful sky, looking for you; where are you now? So lost without your lust. I'm sitting here in this dark, fall night, many broken dreams, heart just beating, looking in the sky, waiting to see you smiling, I'm sitting here in this dark, fall night for you once again to help me through these troubling times, my love, without you, I'm sitting here in this dark, fall night. Where are you now? I know this was more than love, it wasn't no fantasy. I'm sitting here in this dark, fall night; I traveled so far with this bleeding heart, dying so slow inside. I'm sitting here in this dark falling night, but my heart is going down a broken road without you, love. I'm sitting here in this dark, fall night, where are you, my love? This life isn't the same without you. I'm so much broken, it can't be fixed. I wish you were here, saving me from so much. I'm sitting here in this dark, fall night... lying under this falling sky, feeling like this isn't life, not being without you. I'm sitting here in this dark, fall night, where are you now, my love? Times are just getting harder without you. I'm never letting go; you're still a part of me, my once. Love To be. For me to lose something that was part of me, I'm feeling so weak, but not giving up, my love. I'm sitting here in this dark, fall night; I am going crazy. Where are you, my love? I Can't sleep; I keep looking out my window at the sky; I can't find you, my love, that just passed; I hope that you are not fading.

I'm sitting here in this dark, fall night;

I'm watching you fading farther every night. I'm just going to keep walking, even having a bleeding heart until I see your star again.

I'm sitting here in this dark, fall night,

Where I'll be lying once again with my love in this dark sky night....

I Can't Survive

My love, how can survive here without your love, not being able to have you in my world; upside down, my spine so cold, so alone, having nothing but hurt; dying slow inside, alone. I'm not sure how to love without you to show me how; I never felt love until you; never had a love gone, making me cry, as I can't find my way to you. My love, can't be so lost without feeling so cold, so alone in this world; we are alone having nothing but pictures….

Our Last Moments

The last moments we had was the last time we cuddled, you telling me, you'll always be here, With be my shoulder in need and always holding me always close to your heart. The last moments we had, Were so true, love. Now, without, it can't be true. We will never get to hold each other Again. The last moments we had now faded,

I wish there was a way I could call you in heaven To just hear your voice once more; to help me get back up. I'm so weak without you. The last moments we had now lost, my love, I'm so hurt, lost, looking out the window at night, hoping, lying in bed cold, holding my pillows, crying with your Pictures. What's the purpose of life? Not same without you lied to me, you said, you would never Leave or break my heart, telling you really love me. Now I'm sitting here, holding nothing but your photos, falling apart; things are the same. Even when I try to move on, to find new love, I'm losing. My mind is how we're something to nothing but memories, wishing this was nothing but a dream. Our love was so strong now fading, with water in my eyes, can't let go, broken, but

Holding on...

Love Is My Addiction

Every night, fall, sitting on this cold floor, drinking, smoking, looking at her old photos of my once loved, the one starting to feel heartless, lost, hopeless with my faith gone; I can't sleep. I've been up for days on, shaking, turning blue. My addiction; I lost my Lord, taking so much hurt, so much pain; my heart stuck with just one when having so many gone through. I've finally stolen a heart to be taken, made me want to feel love again for her only to be taken. She was my all-in love. With her, we had more than one day. When heaven called, even when I tried to protect her, God took my only love, gone, fading farther away from me. Why does this, I feel, hurt me more when trying to get out of this addiction? I'm drowning without water, dying slow. How do I go on with life with so many fears? I'm lost without her, without her here, with me fading. My life might be ending short, having cancer in my blood; my days round up, short in time; she was my end to my heart, won't die with her by my ....

side, kissing my lips. Can't bear without her tearing me, so she is the only light I have to find. I also have a love never-ending; but I still love all the times we had, my love, I wish I had, but wishing for more love before my time ends....

I Lost Love

I'm just trying to hold this tear. Praying For the strength, the more I hurt in love and in stress, standing out of this addiction I have, I'm not beating my addiction. I can't breathe, drowning; I am no longer in my comfort zone. I have no doubt that I will never get freed of these chains that hold my heart on. I feel like my heart has been burned like hot fire; I feel so lost. My feet are so cold and wet, flooded by my tears, I weep for you; My heart feels so heavy and empty, I have no strength without you, my Bleeding heart Dying slowly inside. Nights are long without you and holding onto my pillows at night, wishing it were you, I wish, holding on

to night, not being my pillows alone…

My nights roaming

I feel I don't have her. I'm so at my aloneness, looking at the moon; I just can't get over love having gone to need her to end my pain from being lost without her. My nights roaming, my name Doesn't mean what it used to be. When I was with her, Now fading in this night Without my heart trying to Sweat it out, crying late, hoping Life wasn't so hard without her by My side, knowing that I lost something Special like her in my life. When I finally stole her heart for mine to be crushed and for her to leave me here all alone When I fell for her only to get hurt. My heart without her here, I really loved much, And I really never loved until her; My first love, I really didn't know what It was until her. Now I can't just give it up. I need more of her love. I'm so addicted....

My Life on Its Side

Hello, this is my life, on its side, my world upside, fading velvet love, sorrow, Hurt, missing her, knowing there isn't back, knowing that her holding, fading away. Life going by without her heart, I have no velvet love; So little life without her. I'm not feeling love, so blind without her heart to be taken makes it hurt, so Baby, you're the reason why I tried love; with Out now, I give up. Just want to be alone. Having just had a love, just you, I want no buddy, but just you. Baby, you're the reason why I give love a try now. See you in a better place. Without my memory fading away from the one I loved, my heart won't let you go. Baby, my love, so Alone, having nothing but hurt, dying slow inside. Hello, my life is on its side; so sad. With her, my only love gone, fading farther away, my only one with velvet love disappearing, Forever lost. My passion forever lost; My love forever and ever. I love forever, lost without her; lost, broken dreams. When I tried to love, to being hurt Without her, Alone, again.... having tried, to hurt without her. Lost without Her in these arms I loved to be taken…

My Love Will Never Be Gone

My love will never be gone; doesn't matter how far you are, my love will never end. It doesn't matter how many miles you are; I will always love. My love will never be gone, even if I have no one to call my own, even when I already gave my heart to someone who is not here. Every day, I'm fighting to hold every day I hope to see you being in the sky, looking down on me, the only time we spend with each other is only in the night where I see you in the sky, shining down from heaven that causes me pain, having no future with you, having my heart ripped out, already missing you. It's causing me so much pain, being the loneliest without you here.

Heaven Can't Wait

Heaven calling, my love having gone to a place where it's bright lighting as star in this sky Don't know what to say; every breath I take without my love, my heart spilt in two lonely parts without her; it doesn't feel right to have a love never getting to be with. I'll never forgive myself for not having strength; losing my love for being short on time, she walked in my life feeling like a nightmare, wishing I was just dreaming, already miss her. It's going take time heal a broken heart, wishing she was here. I've been crucified, wishing I had her. I've been waiting for her, even when I get older, I can't stop loving her. I want to feel love again but only to be without me. Memory never fading away from me, love, this a waking of my once love. I'm right here, waiting for my soul mate to be with. I wish it wasn't late of being in love with her; we were just learning to grow. She was my end to my heart, never healing your heart

won't fill without my love having gone, always feels like she's in my mind. Every night I try to hide how I feel; I can't breathe, drowning without her here to pull me out, my love having gone, wishing I could hold her until her ending; why can't I breathe, trying not to give up without my love gone....

When I Cry

My love crying is the way my heart speaks; when lips can't bear without your love having gone. I love you were good to me, showing what was love for being a short knowing. My heart is barely following, feeling of my once loved; my heart won't let you go. I felt love being in denial, being young, now being loneliest. Every night, I feel I'm dying slowly, having no love; having gone, wishing I was just letting you know I love you. My life not knowing if I was to be with you, to be without you, love, having an empty heart won't let you go. If I wish, I could have just told you how much more I just love you, all deeply feeling so alone; raining days like this aren't real, still think of you, once my love, wishing I told you I love so much. Hurt's gone, leaving my side, being my love, not knowing if you were my soul to be Gone Hurts without you; it's just an angel, crying, late to my knees, my heart never healing. Your love is gone to me to be a loner. When I cry, when you get a little life so shattered, with you having a chance to be without, you got a little more, wishing for you deeply to be here, holding me, keeping always close to your heart...

To My Love

My love, Know I will always love; My love, you will always have my heart. My love, I know you are watching from above. I wish I could move on and find a new love, someone to hold on to during these cold, dark nights. My love in heaven, it's so rare, so pure for me give my heart to someone new; A new love to move on with because you still have my heart. My love, When I look into the stars at night, thinking about us, and wishing we could hold each other just one more time. My love, you're always in my heart, and I will always hold on to what we had....

I Pray

I pray to God the more I hurt in love, in stress, standing outside feeling cold, out of my body; last thing remembering I wasn't feeling right, seeing everybody around my body, trying to get me to move. I pray to God the more I hurt in love, in stress, given so many times to live, having so many loves in life; have to be strong, pray for strength to fight off this cancer that's running through me. I pray to this Lord; He answers by sending me bright angels to wipe tears running down my face while I'm shaking at this mirror, watching my soul go back, knowing that this is a chain to all my memories going to be without stress, broken love, having so much… my life, not so much hurt, so alone; it can't be fixed. I tried. My life is fading with no warning…

Honestly

I'll give you some honesty, lying here with a hallow chest in this big bed alone, wishing she was here. I'll give you some honesty, holding on to my pillows, wishing for a longer time in this world I'm in. I'll give you some honesty, I got you on my mind every second; every breath I take without you, I'm going out of my mind. I'll give you some honesty, lying here, waking up without you, so damn broken. My life is starting not to matter. You are the one I will always love.

I'll give you some honesty, Now I'm alone without my love, lying here with my broken heart, wishing this wasn't goodbye; I'm just being honest. I wish we had more. Waking up without your smiling, give you some honesty, so lost without you, I'm Always feeling so empty, weak, you not being by my side, Lying here wishing it wasn't Nothing but a lie. I'll give you some honesty, my love, I need you here; it's driving me crazy without me holding my love at least one more time. I feel like I can't breathe, I feel…

I can't speak, I feel I can't move, I feel no more.

I feel I'm giving up, I feel life going on without love, I feel I can't be fixed; crying is how I feel. I can't move, cold heart to be alone just because

I can't breathe, trying to stop crying ….

How Do I Deal?

How do you deal with you having a chance of love?

How do you deal with if you had a chance in love for it to be taken?

How do you deal for her, the only one you tried for love to end short?

How do you love to end short?

How do you deal with true heartbreak, getting on my knees, begging God? Just don't take the memories; it's all I have, feeling angels crying from above me.

How do I deal for my love that's gone, watching by my side, helping, wiping my tears away while I lie crying, holding my cold sheets?

How I deal with true love? Hurts lying here, wishing I was just dreaming;

Already miss her much more. I just want it to stop, so more hurt, love less.

How do I deal with true love? Hurts being alone, having nothing but pictures from a long time ago.

I was just in love with her, my love. Can't be so lost without you; my heart won't let you go....

Days Dark and Longer

What am I supposed to do? Days are getting longer in this dark life, having so much pain of losing you. Can't imagine how much I really miss you, looking at you, where my life is now, fading away with us, with all we had, with much chemistry; going out of my mind every second, I have this thought. I wish I could have just sold my soul to have you back. I know you are my star now in my life with no end in pain, my heart, and I'm stuck with just telling you we will see each other one day. I have so much love; I didn't have time to show you when you were my love....

My Life Without You

My life is fading farther from a boy who was always a loner. Stress is a chain that I never get over; being poor, always having strength, but losing my mind, lining myself to feel better.

My life is freaking crazy without you, with so much hurt, so many nights looking out for You;

I gave you a reason, but I can't stop loving you. My life, not so I'm just not beating; Just listen; my heart won't let you go.

My life, there's isn't no pleasant dream living in These shattered shards of life. Stress is getting harder, further than you can imagine.

How much I loved you, I just lost something

That I never told you are the only one who I'll give my heart with much love. Without you in

My life, There's isn't no road like this without you.

Where my life is on its side, my heart won't

Beat; bleeding love, can't get over you.

I'm lying, dying slowly.

My life is going under, having nothing; having no love, having broken down this broke soul to ...

End short, being so blind without you My life,

Being poor in this cold, dark basement;

Started to be a loner going in the deep end

Of this life. I'm so sick. There's a distance of

My once loved one for my heart ending young.

My life, please save me before I fall. Without my first, I just lost my love, poor, cold in this basement, my life so broken without love. Please, I know, please, save me—I'm drowning

Without you, my love, My life,

A loner poor in this basement is a chain;

That is the only light I have. No velvet love, so

Little life, so much hurt, so many nights,

Crying, wishing some way down from this dark

Road that I'm on, walking without you.

My life is gone, and I'm chained down....

I'm So Scared of Love

I'm so scared of love, how it can fold so fast, even when I was so deeply in love.

I'm so scared of love; there's nothing but hurt and no one to hold. So many times, I have been in love, just to be too hurt. I'm so scared of love. I finally gave someone my heart to bleed in,

Hurt for so many nights. I'm so scared of this love, being so cold, holding onto what's left of my love, once so full now, so empty, so weak. Without her love, I'm falling in this fear, and my love life is ending. I'm so scared of my once love now lost, knowing nobody loved me more than she did, my heart bleeding more. She was my first I gave My heart, My love; To end it short being so blind of my first time love.

Can't Live Without You

I told you I never let go, but I lost you and my heart, In the same night, crying late to find true love, lying here hurts more; I gave you my heart,

My life with no water, so weak, turning to the fact I can't stop loving you Isn't a crime because I have fallen in love, now realizing that you are my angel. My life is not so far without you, my love,

Can't sleep well; you're gone its tossing, turning, looking so cold and Holding nothing but the Pillow late through so much pain, being your shoulder to cry for me to be alone, to just so in love with you; There isn't any more tears; I'm lonely, broken, and lost myself in this shattered mirror, Watching my soul go away from me ....

To My Always Love

My love, my always That always speaks my heart on fire. My love, my always, I'm so lost, and it's my beginning; It's starting to fade away.

My love, my always,

My life stuck here without your life, not knowing

We didn't have time to make love one more time

Before God's bidding. My love, my always,

Watching you fly away when I close my eyes at night, hoping, praying for my love to come back to me. My love, my always, it's getting harder, we being further apart; You're fading. Every night, I cry late, hoping to have you holding me.

My love, my always, I'm trying to be strong; haven't seen you to make love one more

time before, I never got to hold you for one more night. My love, my always, crying late to find, hoping for true love; It hurts lying here, waking up, broken up without you. My love, my always, having gone crying, writing, 3:00 in the morning, Knowing I lost you, my heart has no beat; it's hard to be. My love, my always, in so many nights, cold, holding my pillows, crying late, hoping to have you holding me,

My love, my always, Keeping me always close. Now our life is fading farther away with my life on this cold floor in My dark corner, crying, knowing it's too late to be with the one who has my heart, and now it's gone...

Getting Older

Dear my love, sitting right here by this cold window, getting much older, waiting for you to come back to my life going on without you, it's just getting harder, thinking of you. I can't wait anymore, I was hoping it never slips away, feeling it's so real; I can't put it up without you. It's cold in my bed, chills going through me right next to where you laid now. My life and my only, it's my time; I am not going on without you were my reason, why I need you here....

I Have to Do This

I have to do this on my own. I have to. I have so much hurt; I have no feeling to love anymore. I have a tragic life I'm living in, not having nobody, trying to give a try to find true love. I hope to see it so soon. I'm watching my scars, bleeding. More love, can't stop; I have no velvet to my life. I have to find true love.

"LOVE" IS LIKE ROSE'S

Red rose of our Love Bringing me to life with love in the air, and living like a pair of roses in spring; So much red, So much love, So much we grow in pairs to comeback once a year to get growing older and die with each other as a pair that always met in the spring, To Pair In Life Like A Red Rose, As We always grow with each other to grow old with and die with each other, with so much love…

I cannot escape

I can't escape what could have been, I can't escape your grasp, I can't escape having those chains so tight to my heart, I can't escape feeling so alone, weak, tossing and turning, feeling the withdrawal. I can't escape this love, my first; it hurts. Just didn't know what I started, but here is so much pain. I started to get numb. I can't escape; I just think of her as I'm losing it all, deeply feeling so empty without her ....

Never Be Easily Replaced

I know it's not your fault; I don't know how to love. I know how much you taught Me about love and what it means, opening my mind, getting lost, my heart being so hypnotized, needing Curling from your love, knowing you'll Never be easily replaced with all of the time we have left...

My Love

My love, know I always love you. My love, I know you own my heart. My love, know that even though you're above watching, I have to move to find love so I can hold through the nights being so cold. My love, it's hard to give someone else the rest of my love, to fall in love again when I gave you Most of my heart. My love, I always look to your star every night, going on until We get hold each other once more.

I Gave and Lost

I gave my love and lost my best friend, My everything , my You filled my life with sunshine and so much happiness. My love, when you were here walking this Earth with me, it was my best moments. I really will cherish you and hold on.

My best friend, now that you have gone and left this Earth, my heart feels so lonely and alone, Wandering the streets without you. My everything, I'm walking on this very ground that we want to walk together, missing and Longing for you to be back with me and bring me back sunshine to fulfill my heart that's filled with sadness without you, my love. I made a promise to always be with you....

Me and My Love

My baby, if my baby dies; I die, too. My baby cries,

I cry with my baby lies, I lie, too. If she's sad,

I'm sad, too. She's my friend I'm her friend, too. She was my wish; She is all I need. She is my only one heart, one love, one life, one I only need. My baby dies, I die. If she cries, I cry, too.

If my love lies, I lie with her. If my baby's sad,

I'm sad with her. She'll always be friends;

I will never let her go. She will always be my love until my end, my friend, my everything until are last breathe....

Before My Hourglass Ends

You already know what I'm on.

Days going on with me going through so much pain, with cancer running through me,

I'm so scared. Looking at this hourglass that is running out, having no love, being so scared I'll never put that ring on her before my time is up.

I just have so many scars; I hope they never show. No matter how much more pain I'm in, I just want to love before it's too late. I need your love; I can't do this by myself, looking at time, hoping it's not too late without love.

My hourglass is half gone, starting to stiffen, being so scared of death and not being able to find true love. Lying here hurts more; I hurt in having no love that holds me before I go.....

My heart filled

With hurt, some like your love storyline,

it's tragic, l got filled with hurt feelings and scars that will never heal. But open bleeding wide open, When I gave her my heart, that will never heal, when I lost her, I I'm lost parts that can't get replaced, when she made me feel like I wasn't there, she made me feel like I wasn't enough, Even when I gave her my heart Just To Lose.

I couldn't even have the thought of me losing her; It's like I'm stuck in a nightmare; She's not there. I'm in so much pain; Tears Keep Running;

The Thought I'm lost In, A love, for long and ever Fading away From Me. Love gone, I never wanted to lose....

Not to a Stranger

I don't want to give my heart up, not to a female bunny anymore stranger when I know I already gave it to you. Even though I know you're far, but choose here in my heart, you always be in My heart; I'll never give it up to a bunny stranger. To hurt more inside when I already gave all my love to you, I have no more to give. My heart, it's on empty. I just can't live without you here beside me anymore...I'm alone and can't just give my heart to a stranger, When I already gave it to you, my love....

My Cinderella Life

My life stuck around darkness, My life is in a bad fairy tale, So broken; there isn't no ending young, having no princess, In my Cinderella, Life going on, I Would sell my Soul, but just don't have one.

I don't want to be alone, having just been out of... my first relationship For me to be heartless with This bleeding love, living in this fairy tale of my life with no end, in pain, my life with no feeling of love again.....

Her Photo

You don't have to ask why I hurt so much inside. Every time I look at her photo, wishing that she was here in my life, in my arms, my only love, memories took deep inside, close to my heart. Even though we're far apart, every day I always imagine even though our love will never disappear in this dark shadow that follows me every day, I will always believe searching for the light to bring us closer. In my hopes and dreams, that will never change, my love I have for you, when I'm without you, my life is fading farther away from reality.....

When I Cry for You

When I cry, not having your love to wipe tears away sadly, nor so sad, I don't want to believe I lost my love.

When I cry, it's with so many fears that I lost my heart, now just pain, having no love, having an hourglass. This pain is so real.

When I cry, there isn't no pleasant dream, living the life you left behind. When I cry, telling myself you're gone, feeling so cold, so alone

When I cry, so lost; look at sky, hoping to have you come home, Help me back up; losing my Mind how we were something to nothing but memories, Wishing this wasn't goodbye. So much love, so much hurt. There are so many scars, so I'm so broken up without your love …

You on My Mind

My life's hard; If I would lose you, how you mean to me Is Really One of kind. How you're always running on my mind, How you brighten my life with warmth, How I couldn't wish for a better friend, How I'll pick you in millions, How I'll never let go, How you'll be My Love Forever....

Not Having a No Buddy

Once lost, I felt just for lust to fall in love, not knowing what it was to have, wishing I was in a transition to a new life I wasn't ready for. Once just lost, feeling I can't move on to her; I'm sorry. For the first time, I was just letting her go without having so many in my life, feeling just lust, not love, it's my life now fading farther away from me. Once my first love now gone far; without her, only hurt. Hit by love, without her, it tears me apart; my heart on fire. So lost, So much velvet, My once loved heart never healing right without my first love darling, She is the reason why I tried Love. Now she's gone to leave me alone, having nothing to hold but these memories. I have to go to a place where it's not love; it's my health going belly up. I need you here. Where are you? just don't l For you to end it short. True love, I guess for you to end it short…

I'm So Without You

I'm so Damn broken with my life being so shattered without my love Having so many regrets. I'm so hurt that I never told how I felt, wishing I could go back, knowing how lucky I was to have you. I'm so hurt that she's not around. having so much love for you, Wishing I could go back in time to fix things, as I'm so Broken that I don't have her holding me at night, where there'll be no darkness, just someone I Used to love. I'm so sick. There's a distance that I used to be so broken, my life lonely with no love, without nothing, without the one I want to be with. I'm so lucky to have a love like her in my life. Now, I'm lost, and it's erasing all the times we had. I'm so in love, don't know why I keep looking in the sky, but I can't stop; She's the one and there's No embarrassment or hiding it: She is the one. I will never stop until I get to hold her at least once again. I'm so glad to have had a wonderful person and spent 5 percent of my life with me. She was my picture of a thousand words, wishing I could go back to fix it so I can be with my love again…

When I See You

My heart gets warmer. When I see you, my life always turns around. When I see you, I can pick you up in millions. When I see you, I hope for more sanity. When I see you, I wish I could be the one to hold your hand. When I am by myself, I am looking for my right to show me how to love again, hoping it to be you. Without my first love now gone, Siegen answers to the light of the first time I saw my little secret My true love....

It Hurts You're Not Coming

Why it hurts the most to get that call that your love's not coming. As it's hurts the most, knowing you're now alone as are feels start fade are love that's gone, and it can't be fixed. A Crying, as she left with no warning., it hurts the most; you left me alone, An I know you're gone, feeling so cold, so alone, so blue; she Is gone. it hurts the most, she's watching me cry as an angel, now mine., it hurts the most; I need her here, where you just don't know how much I loved you; I just lost Something there, not a replacement that I never told her how I'm losing my mind, How I felt, wishing I could go to a place we met. it hurts the most, having nothing like her, my heart just not beating, my mind racing, drowning in these tears, all because of her. I need you here with me, fading. It hurts the most, my love disappearing; so, lost without you.

My life is freaking crazy without you,

My love disappearing, so lost, knowing nobody was going be her, My first love now gone, Siegen, Answers, crying late, hoping I can find my way to her heart. She never told me bye; Oh, it hurts the most. Why'd she leaves me? My heart, so sure, I'm beginning to love you. It hurts, and there's no one to save me; you're not to save me from, So much hurt, so much broken heart. I wish I had someone to hold. It's hard; It's hurts to be alone having just been crucified, wishing I had someone to hold in this dark, fall night, crying for above, hardly breathing; I beg, it's driving me crazy. Without you, I got cold in the deep end to my love.

So Many Moonlights

My love, I can make you rich in love, holding you in so many moonlights. My love disappearing, so lost, knowing nobody loved me like you did.

My love, I just want to hold the thought of losing you since I could never be without you. My love, I would have so much hurt, so many scars, so broken up, angel, without your heart, won't let out; life going by without you, feeling so empty, weak, turning, losing my love. I just lost a best friend, lost with in my love gone, fading farther away from me. Love, this wasn't goodbye;

so many nights, cold heart, she can find me meaningful with my heart. Won't let her go without her tearing or die with in my life, I'm only hurting, trying to give a damn, broken with my love gone, fading away from me. Love that always speaks, my heart won't let her go with all my memories, holding her through the nights, hoping it will last forever, lost without my lover....

I Can't Forget You

When I am by myself, looking in this mirror, watching the tears fall, seeing my love's reflection, feeling like I fell in love at the wrong time in this life. When I'm by myself with a broken heart that's been crucified with a nail on each side without my blood, barely Following, feeling so empty. When I'm by myself with having no heartbeat sitting in this dark corner, can't stop the pain I'm having, can't stop thinking of my once love, Not having the strength to move on, always thinking of her. When I'm by myself, it's not fair; I never told her how much she meant, holding her picture to my heart, never getting a chance to say goodbye. So many nights crying, wishing some way down the line, I get to run into my love, so there will be no more goodbyes. When I'm by myself, I wish I could get to hold her at least one more time, being so many raining days and nights without her.....

Goodbye

This is goodbye; I think we fell in love just at the wrong time. I hope we meet again somewhere down these dark, crazy roads were on. We just needed more time. I think of you every night, crying late, wishing you hadn't ended, trying not to break any promises yet to get to run into my love again. My love, there isn't no happy in ever ending young, having me drowning in Missed Love by my side for my soul to end. My once love left me alone; there is no blame, it's not going on without my life. Without you. my Heart's starting to fade away and next to you, my love, I can't sleep. I've been up for days missing you. My only love having gone, crying, writing to you, my once love, to my heart to be taken makes me Want you more....

I hope to see Morning Light

I hope to see morning light every time I close my eyes; I'm not ready for heaven. I'm calling even though my life is fading. I hope to see morning light. When she was my shadow to my life, now fading farther away, I hope to see morning light.

Like the star fading away, every night, I won't let go; broken but holding on to what's fading

I hope to see morning light. Fading farther, hoping Heaven isn't calling with life fading further without my love in my corner, I hope to see morning light. Every time I close my eyes, hoping that I see the sun rise, Hoping I missed heaven calling one more night To find my love once to be before the hourglass runs out hoping love will be with me, once again.....

I'm So Hurt Without Love

I'm so used to love, I'm so used to holding a hand, I'm so used to walking in sand, singing to you with our feet wet. I'm so used to holding on to you, watching the stars; I'm so used to you, doing so much with you. I'm so used to being hurt by the ones I always gave my heart to.

I'm so used to crying over you every night in pain and stress in my chest. I'm so used to being alone, never getting over you. I'm so used to being down in this life of darkness. I'm so used to having so much to end, nothing in everything I try to prove; I'm so used to nobody wanting me.

I guess I'm just disappointed I don't have a life....

When Love Split in Two

Ever since our lives have split apart, our souls are so lost, walking around as a zombie, so gone with our lives that are split apart. Now, we're both alone, and it hurts that we're both so lost. When loves lost, separated from one Another, drifting through life with no Feeling, lost without your love my life has Been a roller coaster with its ups and downs, twists and turns, at times, lost not, knowing which end is up. Being used to walking these streets, alone growing up being poor, my life on a roller-coaster, never knowing where I am at; Where does my life end of this hurtful story I'm going through? Holding on, pushing through the pain at times too hard to bear, So many cold nights without your love, Holding onto the memory of you while my Head spins, wanting you with me; barely Holding on to sanity, being so scared I'll Never get off this roller-coaster I'm on, alone.....

My Life With So Much

My life with no end in pain, Going on with no end, I'd rather run but have nowhere to go.

My life with no end in pain to be lonely, trying to hide in this dark shadow close to the light.

My life with no end in pain, my head spinning, drowning in the sand with no water. My life with no end in pain, Feeling So weak, turning blue; she was my end to my beginning. My life with no end in pain, I'm drowning without her here to pull me back to life, going on without her here. My life with no end in pain, tearing me apart; my heart on fire, now cold, not beating just listen. My life with no end in pain, my love having gone far too long, not knowing if she was the perfect one for me. My life with no end in pain with my love in a small ending. My life with no end in pain Becoming so numb I can't move with my cold heart. My life with no end in pain, lying here, waking, crying in pain, knowing I can't live without my love not being around. My life with... no end in pain, just in my dream, feeling so real; still hear the voice whispering in my ear. We're playing hide and seek She knowing how much I love her when I let her go, wishing for her to be Here, lying with me in this cold night without but within a fall, raining night ....

Love

My wish Come true, Dear darling of

Mine, I could never find a better love. A true friend, A wish come true; Love that I'll always cherish. Dear my friend, I was at my end to make this wish to have you in this world where the water runs dry. Dear my love, it's been days since I was holding you, but I know you're shining down from heaven up for Days, missing the love we had, always looking for light Dear angel of Mine, It's been years since I was holding you, but I know you're lost, broken, my life so broken, Love, having So much pain, being loneliest....

I miss the love we had, even when we were so much more. I just lost my friend, my love, having just an angel, my only love…

If I could

If I could bring you back, I would sell my soul. You are the reason why I tried love without you. My love gone with nobody to love me like you once did, my love, you are the only one who I love. And I'll never leave. You are my reason why I tried love. What am I supposed to do without you here? I'm Mr. Lonely without my girl of my dreams. Everything I do reminds me of you;

I can't get over you; I'm lying, dying slowly inside. It hurts with this pain, having no future in this dark love of my once love life. Your love is addictive. Was our love real? With you gone, it's not fair to our life, now fading away from me, love. This life ripped my heart, never healing. Your love is so strong, without my lover, my life just to end, no one calling my phone.....

My love is dying slowly in this world. We are just not the same without having so many regrets that I'll never be able to hold her until her ending in this dark world. My love, I'm hurting, trying a fake life to the fact I have no velvet To be without you, love, we were supposed to live our life, But ending young, being short; just hope you can find me. I'm being meaningful for you, my love, It can't be true; you were my life, not to die in a short time. It was my end to my love. There never will be another; She was my shadow to my life, now I'm alone in This empty room. My mysterious Lover My lifetime best friend…

My surrender to my beginning, I'm dying slow inside. It is what I am without my love, having no one to save me, having my guard down until we meet again. I'll fall in love once more, holding her in these cold nights...

Feeling Heartless

Nobody deserves to hurt from love, how much can my heart take, being glass so easy to break? And starting to feel heartless, having so many regrets in this life, giving my heart to fake love to say goodbye; it's not fair, trying to find love, not war. Try to find real happiness, even if it really exists. Having so much wrong, not meeting real love, having no more trust in love; I don't want to do this anymore. It hurts more when I say love.

It hurts with my glass heart that shattered,

Never being the same, not being used to love, always hurting ....

I'm Tearing Apart

I'm not doing fine; without you, I feel my life going by with all my memories going with it. I feel nemesis from so much hurt, so many scars, it's taking too long to heal....

I feel so alone in this world, even when I stand with millions, being so alone nobody notices.

I feel like it's always raining, every minute I'm living, trying not to get hurt, But the more try I still get hurt, so why try anymore to just get hurt? I feel I do nothing but try, but I always hurt, dying so slow. If it's not love, it's my health getting worse, I feel I've been going through this for far too long. When will it just change? My sun will never rise with so much silence. With my life fading in this darkness, I feel pettier. Every time I fall asleep, she gets taken by cops and then to our Lord; I feel I can't breathe, trying not, letting go to my love. I'm trying to be strong, but I'm so broken, I'm feeling so alone, having no more heart on this sleeve, I feel like it will never end, never, no; when this life going, being short, I just hope everybody knows, I promise I did nothing but try, Feeling like I'm under water, and I'm not letting go to my loved one....

Walking With a Fake Smile

I'm so sick, crying late, hiding behind my smile, always acting like my life is okay when inside, I'm dark with hurt, feeling with scars, knowing that I can't by myself look in this cold window, hoping my life is fading farther from my demonstration, losing my mind, lining to myself to be alone, just so I hurt some more, crying out the window, tears flowing like a cold river, holding my pillows like it was someone I used to love. It seems like my life will never change; I'm so sick of crying, hiding behind my smile that's so fake, hurting so much inside. I let my guard down; this broke my soul to be without you; can't hold on anymore. I hurt the more I cry. The days go without having so many regrets in this dark life; doesn't matter. I can't breathe, drowning in hurt, being so sick, having so much going wrong my life. It's on an hourglass; it's running fast, knowing I can't stop. It's going to die with me feeling like I can't breathe, drowning in this sand without you......

When the One I Loved Is Gone

When the one I loved is gone, is she still with me or fading to the light of my once love life? I'm looking in the mirror, not recognizing who's staring back and feeling tears roll down this broken soul. Can't love anybody. What am I supposed to do? I can't get over you; my only my life, not meeting nothing like this. This isn't real, crying late, wishing it wasn't true. I lost you lost within my heart, never heal my mind; every night, never being able to hold her until her life just to be taken. She was My Only, My Heart, My Love, My Friend, I'm lost without feeling like I have nobody to love; just lonely, broken inside. It hurts with pain. Having no love having gone, wishing hope for her, only to be without my memory fading away. From my love, this girl, I just lost her; without her heart to be within my life. feeling broken up, angel, without your love.....

My Time in Life

There was a time I never felt pain, and there was a time I never loved. There was a time in my life when I was unstoppable, playing football ball, and it ended with an eighteen-wheeler. There's a time when I'm on my third life, just trying to find my way. There was a time in my life when I finally found love for it , in tragic pain that I'll always have. There's a time in my life feeling broken being without feeling I'm not somebody. Now's there's a time in my life I'm tired of being in this nightmare I'm in, asking for strength to fight off this cancer that's running in my veins. I'm not being lucky, I have nobody to save me if I'm in pain.

My life is always putting me at set back; I can't get over with the words to be always in my heart, and I will always echo ...

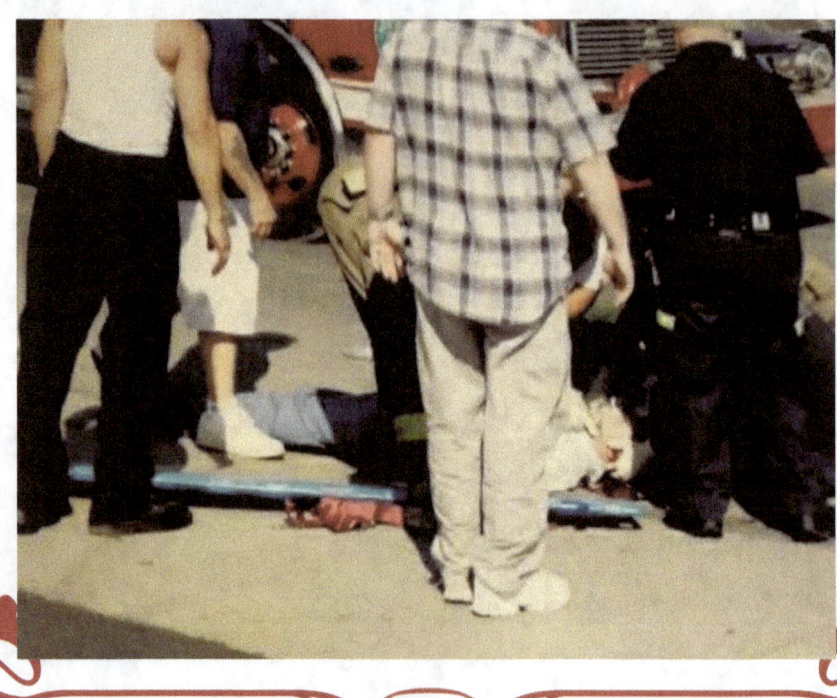

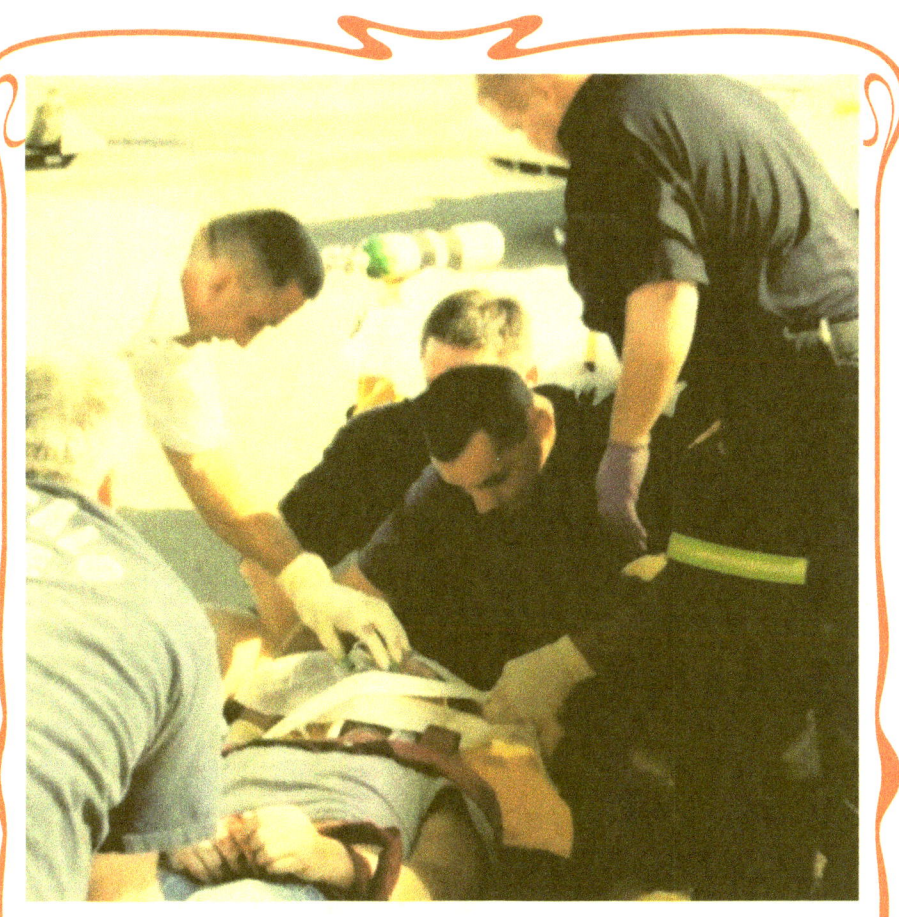

To always try to fall forward, but to always fall in a bad day. That always turns in a dark cloud,

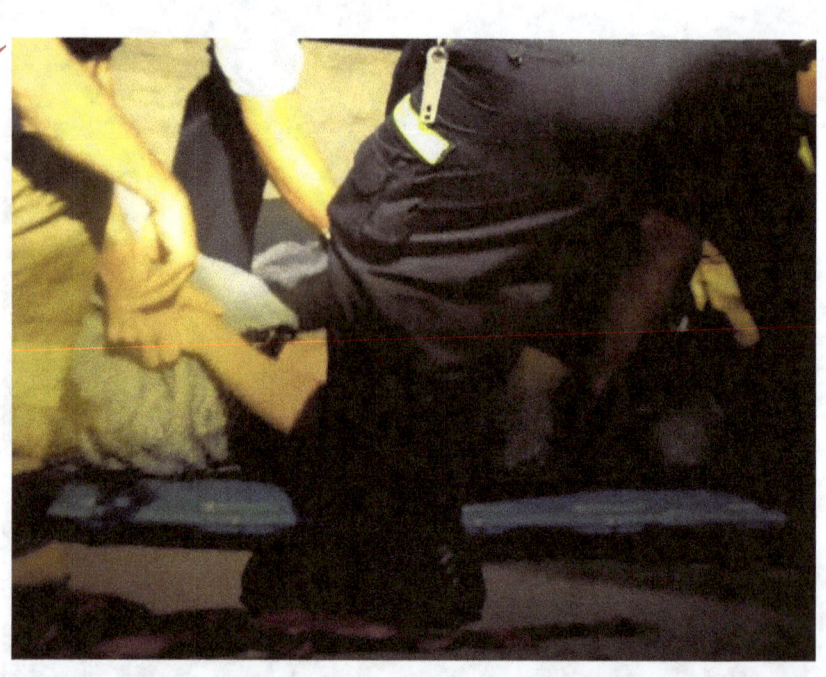

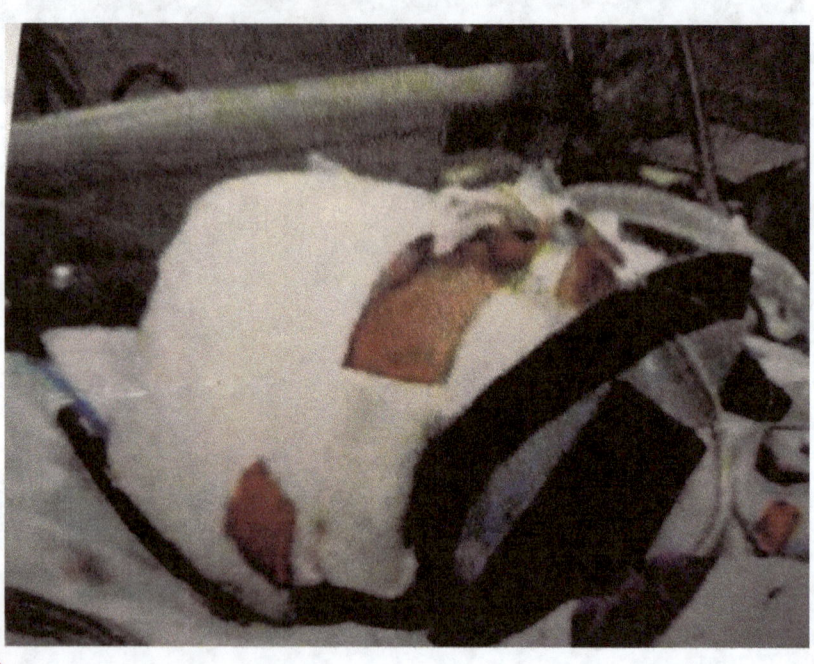

To try to face it, always try to step forward, try to win, never lose, to learn and never forget ....

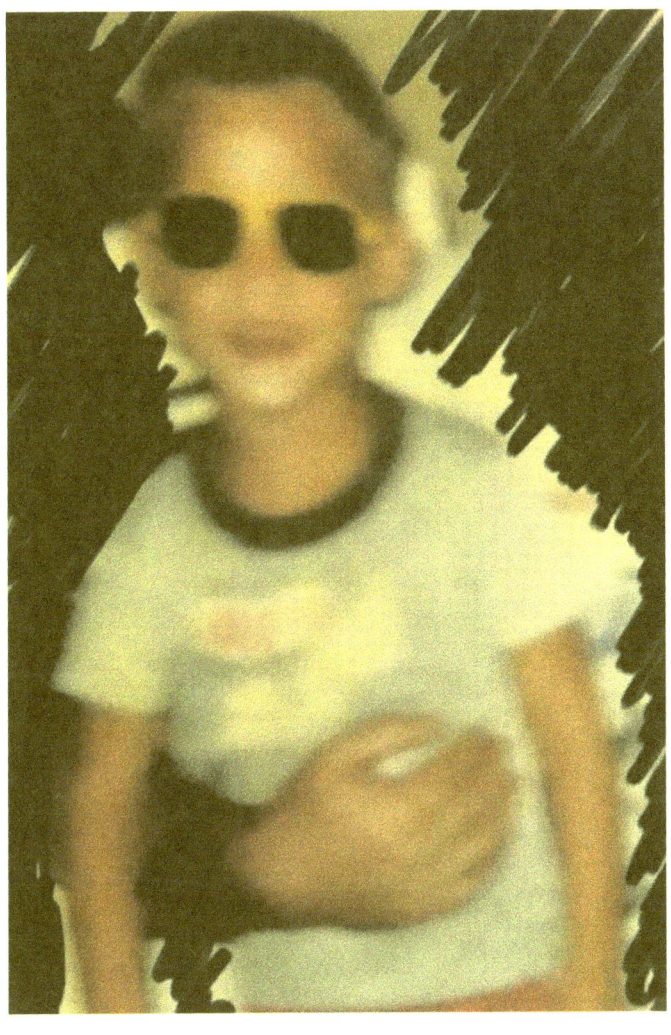

What's always trying to break me with the pain That is temporary, And I know it's not permanent; To know how much you are going through, There is no limit on never giving up,.....

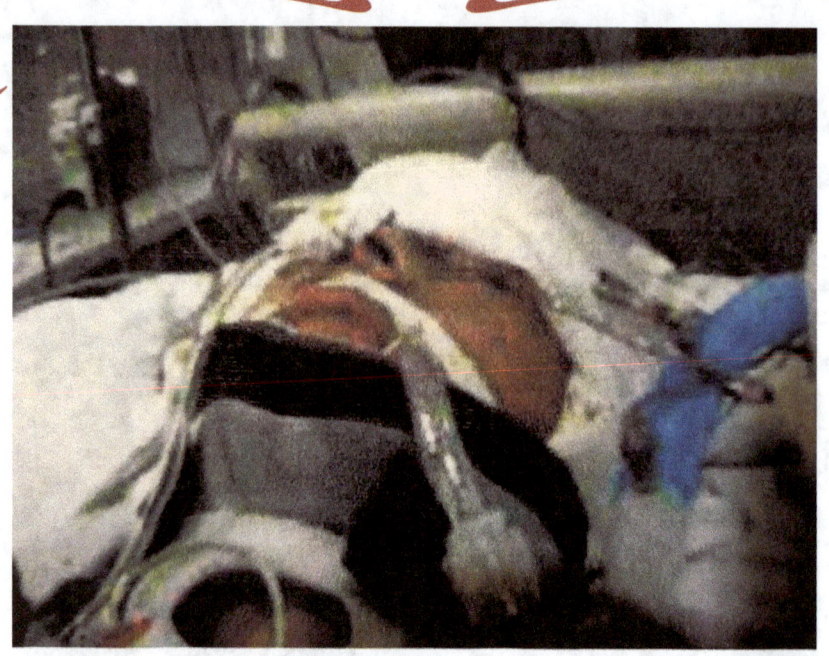

Even through the impossibly from my own experience, always getting back up, With so much pain to get stronger, to always getting Ready to fight and face any situation that comes, To always move forward in my multiversity of pain That always makes me crawl to make an impact in my life. If I save a life or beat cancer Over a love To learn, my life is no game, but for just living,....

To never give up, To always get on with life, Where There's light with uniting To a struggle, and To get back up...

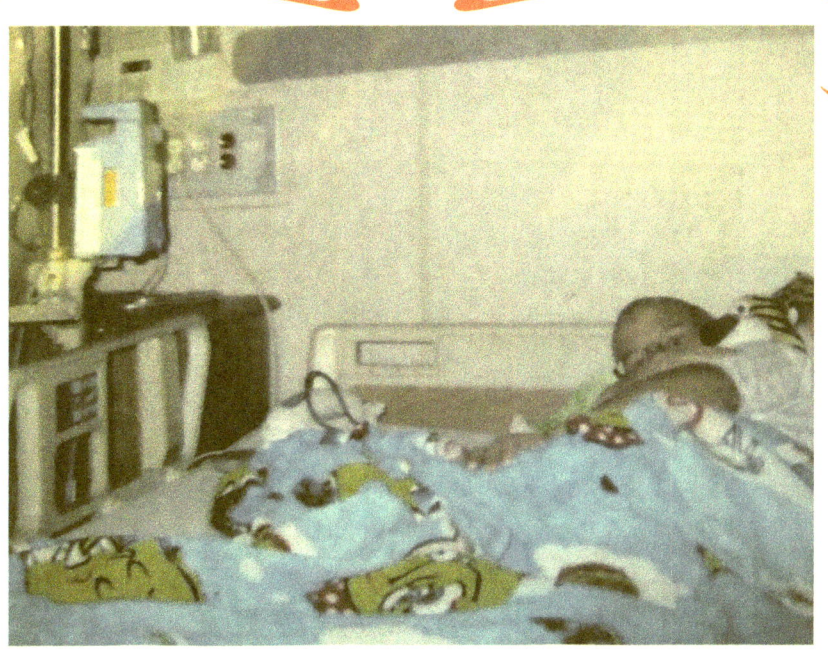

With a full heart, even if I feel there is no reason

To go anymore, To try self-love, To Try not self-hatred, With Life being short, To try make a difference in it, Even if I'm in pain…

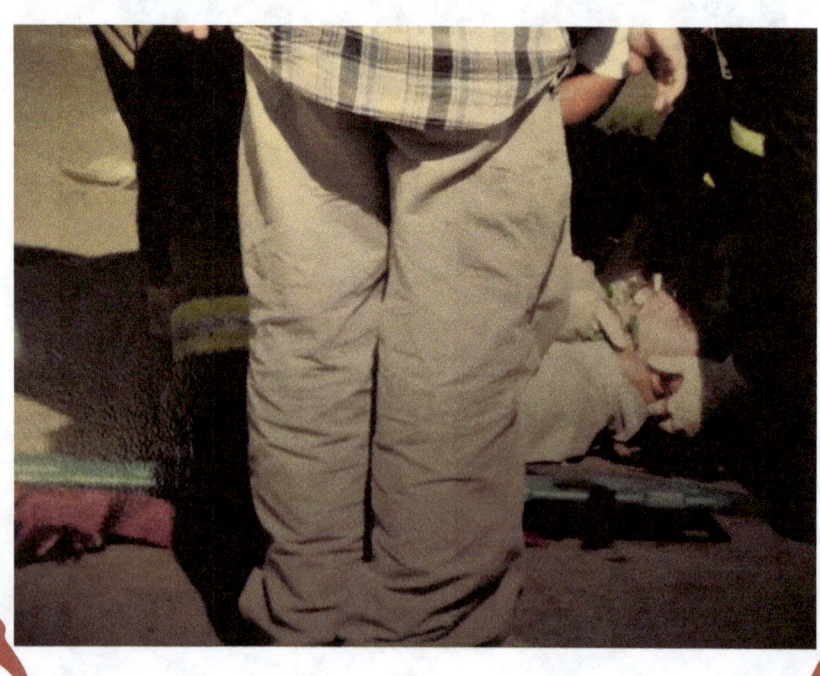

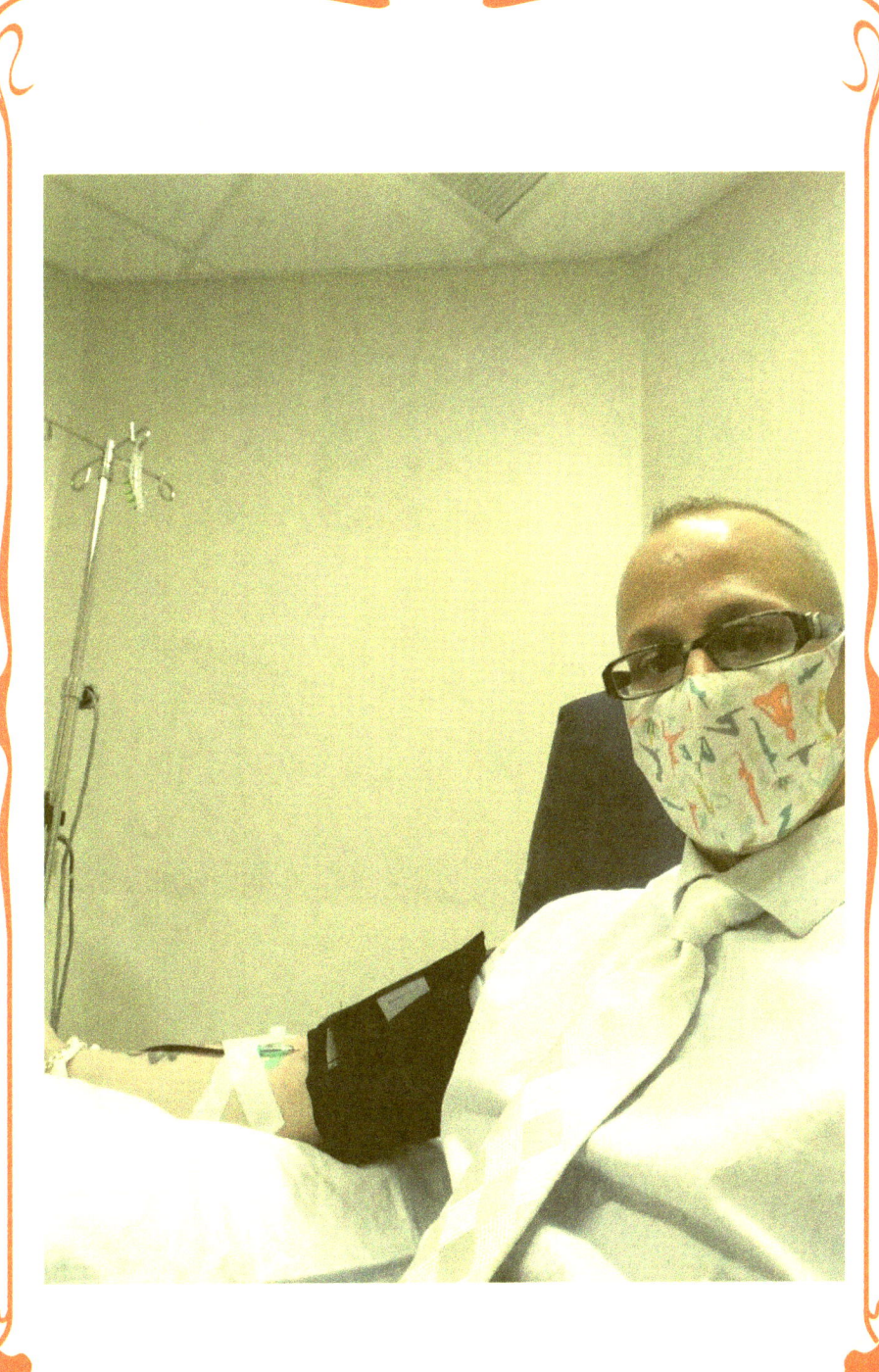

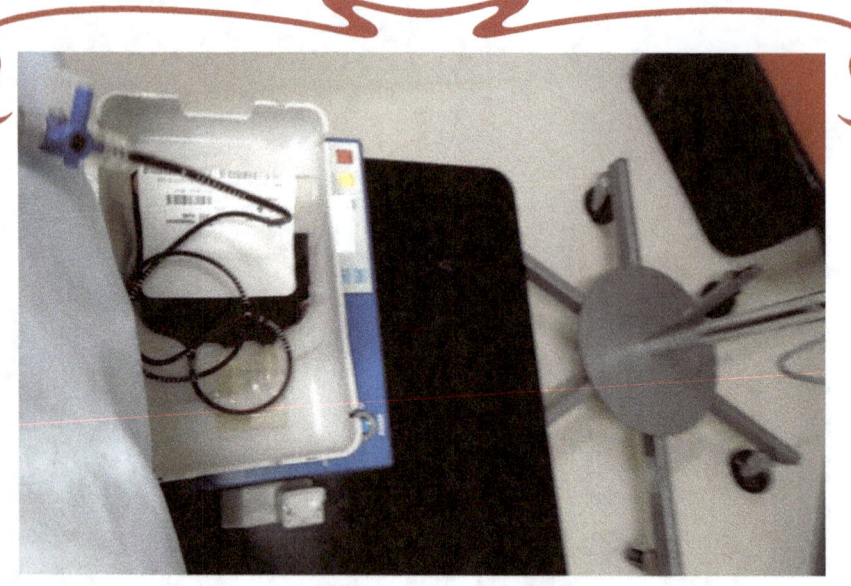
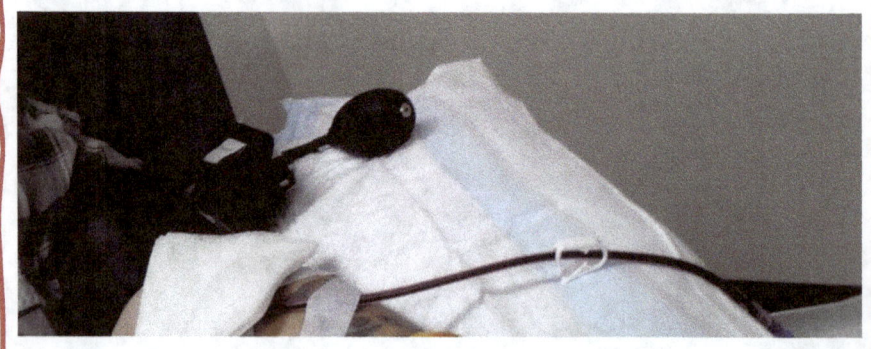
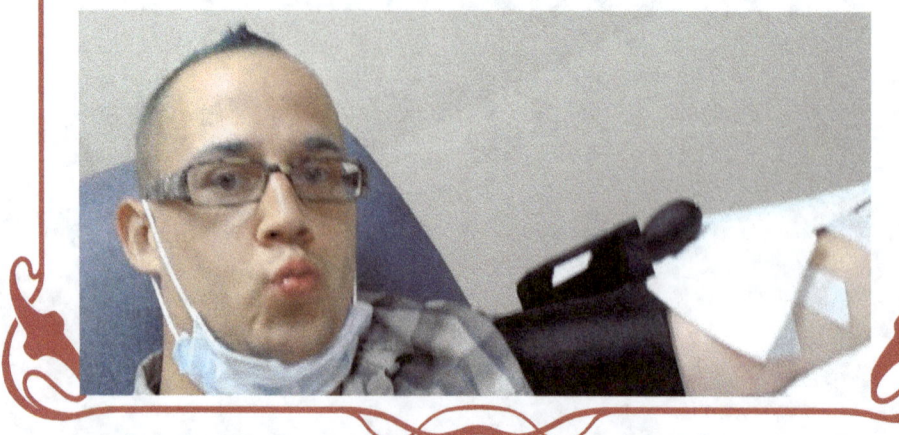

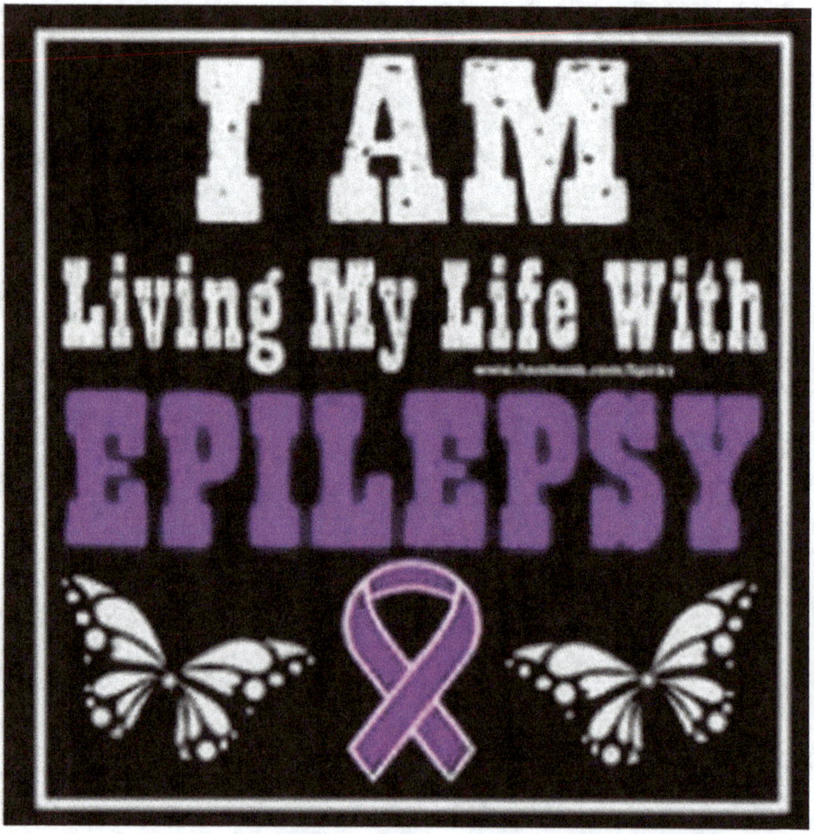
I AM
Living My Life With
EPILEPSY

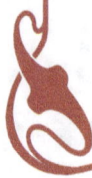

It was a hard time to find my type of woman , that will respect my loyalty, someone I give all my love and swear don't give up so easily locking looking at her knowing she that one coming from my heart and always getting.... Emotional looking at her eyes so perish like glass diamonds shining getting tighter to mine every night As closing my eyes holding her Feeling her every beat getting warmer when touches begins soft lips rub mines That sweet smell behind blowing her ear my lips softly go down driving her I'm driving swerving her back ached giving life another meaning to the sky as are limits the world seeing my diamonds flesh I think I can't get any more better from just a year ago I can't be stuck in the presents she is my future coming up screaming showing no remorse because no one will show as much she will to be praying for more time to now so happy finding my life is all most complete and finally opening these gates that's been locked for most of this life because of I Gregory was nothing more than a night gale it would just start with a drink then waking up alone looking at an empty bottle no one around. I had quite because I took care of hundreds women for a couple hours and then it's alone again sleeping holding pillows to make moves... for that change to feel what is love so happy I found my replacement of this pain an knowing she loves me and holding me every night fall Wishing for nothing more than just A one night teaser in a different way ....

YOU CAN'T TAKE LIFE FOR GRANTED

because you only live once, with my own experience I have learned don't take life for granted because you only live once and never give up even if you're in the darkest paths life throws at you and even if sometimes it feels like no one cares but you it doesn't mean you should ever give up on yourself or listen to people or haters that you ever couldn't find your dreams that hurt too get there and there's no one to be found to help you be found you have to just take what Life gives you, and you will be found. I promise you.

She was my first

that ever lasted more than a day it's been a year and I so glad I tried to make it right so glad that I finally found a love and no more nights alone so glad I found A love more than a dream so glad I found my special someone I can pour my heart into. I got myself off the ground after falling so many times before and having a heart ice cold , where I couldn't take it alone anymore until the day my heart hooked to that special someone as God Finally answered my prayers and gave me my soul mate and an escape from this pain, with having a hard time living with this broken life being so thankful for this special woman for making free opening up these gates to my heart that's been locked away Far too long with her Giving me a love for never had before knowing that I ever love again hoping she knows I still need her case I fall again because no one will ever catch me if I fall down without her I'll never could make it she is more than a friend she is somebody that picks me up even if me thinks it's too late, and she somebody I love even if it kills me slowly knowing I have reason to keep fighting in this life even if cancer she is my reason why my heart keeps beating So many times I have ran away. I just want to say that I'm blessed to have her in my life now .....

As I've realized that I have fallen in love with a sweet escape to know you're more than a friend , and more than just a one nightstand , something I promise I'm done with you are my mission to love you through this life hold you tight through the night and to know if I fall to know you will be there when I Land you will be there when I land but I couldn't tell you the way down but your always here to catch me when needing you're love more then you know to keep fighting even if I never ending to this pain in each of my veins running On fire warming, my cold heart crackles down risk. Being mentally gone atheist to find inter peace being stuck with this cancer until I can't breathe any longer and I'm so proud to have you and be with until my last nights!

I hope you understand. Everyone has left me where I stand now, but not you, I prayed for these days to come true, so I am thankful for her in my life ....

So how can I fix her? if I can't fix myself, I tried to bring you on, but you left me Stranded, so how can I help you? if I'm so broken to? My heart is ice cold, so. how can I fix you? if I can't fix myself, I tried to bring you on, but you left me Stranded, so how can I help you if I'm so broken to? My heart is ice cold, When I take the Blindfold off, you're still not going to be here. You can go. I don't need you here. I'm not going to Chase you anymore, I tried to keep you close, but it never fell through, you know, how we say goodbye we don't need to, you think I need you your wrong I'm doing it like chasing the weather getting worse to the best now without you I loved you like you took my heart for granted because you don't need my love. When I take the Blindfold off, you're still not going to be here. You can go. I don't need you here. I'm not going to Chase you anymore, I tried to keep you close, but it never fell through, you know, how we say goodbye, we don't need to, you think I need you your wrong I'm doing it like chasing the weather getting worse to my best now without you and I loved you like nobody else would, and you took my heart for granted, and I can't ever get it back. I really mean it feeling differently having no rebound over my life sentence I can't bear it anymore watching you dreaming when I'm stuck in reality, check like I should be pages each book in a different way to have her in any weather and I can't take it now. Is it too late and too far away from me to fulfill my broken angel heart won't fill without true Love imploring away, killing me slowly, knowing if I die not from my health but a broken heart. I will have to go with it!

Yes, I'm not the person you used to know. Time is changing, and you can't stop time. How most you ever try, and you can't wait on time because it never stops, the day we stop doing our lifestyle the day we start to fade more away even if we are in pain because you know comes in different ways and we can't never stop or it will be too late and pain will never stop.

Now, this wasn't the plan , but I took that chance, fighting against all odds having my back in the corner alone in the rain standing, writing over 4000 pages , never going to college for poetry, I did this all on bad health Having cancer, Epilepsy an seizures, losing weight Panic attacks, making 900 a month, I wrote 30 books in two years , I have over 100,000 fans around the world in seven different media set's because I never gave up and I hope my writing help others and shows them there is more to life never give up ....

This sweet escape when in pain helps me, especially when falling, and this time, I've never run because I don't know the way down this path grows e'er the more lonely, hungry pain missing I can't disregard knowing this I can feel more and it's hard at times living like being cold in December. And Knowing We all get these hard-hitting reminders of whom you are In times of sadness In times of powerlessness In times when we are left with so many questions, as I'm but a frail bird tasked to bring hope and spread peace.

How shall I fly high in the sky with such a brittle burden! My heart and Sitting on a branch of a white spotted tree Shivering, crying, and alone Away from home, on the highest branch that can hold me Hiding no more beatings It's so hard to look at this mirror and see how much I changed being so blind growing up and going through with so much pain and Agony trying to get through these nightmares that got my heart in pieces because I can't sleep with this pain that has my heart on its knee's wishing I could take this pain away from me that has my heart.

I need you to understand I need you more than you ever I knew with so many that I still don't know my name, but they are just watching me coming from the dirt, rising slowly changing like weather knowing I am having big plans, and I need everyone to believe in me, please.

I promise to be strong, and with the day I stop moving, is the day I started to fade away, and I'm already tired, but to know I worked so hard to be successful in my books and having so much support to my new journey of life.

Whispers in my head, you're not going leave here alive , with my days and nights being nightmares on repeat. I don't know how much I take THERE'S NO PRETENDING feeling Hurting This pain holds me in chains There's no prescription. Even if having nightmares every time I close these eyes, I can't let it break me for many years running from those demons day and nights my soul is tied hoping wishing there is more than this life and not just battling demons hopping out this dark and hoping for light please tell me when does it end lord for years I been running from trauma turning into drama chasing it with bottles of lord feeling I'm losing it again days are getting more hard feeling the lacking getting hard to breath with this chest pain never leaving THAT was sinking in deep frenzied drowning drenching of my heart utilizing the day of my soul out of darkness restless and in light once again because I don't want this pain it's drowning me in this temperature rising and flowing through these veins scattered obsession so tight crying gagging to try and get out of this dreams that's on repeat I promise I'm trying to find my way before it's too late and everything is gone with nobody's else around me; having no morning shine and I don't want to miss out in love and let it set my free watching my Shackles falling chains breaking gates opening up more then you'll ever know! "Pouring my heart out in like these versions I have knowing my darkness will turn in light my heart will be on fire lighting being of my life. In this nightmare life, I battled most of it alone, always staring into the devil eyes as he walked all levels, trying to get me to sell my soul. As most of my life I Walking down these roads alone, feeling a shameful bottled up breaking inside Growing up in a household, 2 brothers and 2 sisters and a mother so broken fighting to be a father to because mine was missing miles and miles away and a family so big but so small of my little hand when I'm here fighting to be more demons come and take with no questions. But I can't help and get back up and try to hold this embrace of pain that will never leave. Being the survival of the fetishist coming from these streets from the day I started to walk until the day use cross my heart, you will see my scars and hear of my wars I lived. Even if I gave, you'll all the love. I didn't live in a happy home life, starting too young now. I learned from the streets, and I grew up and never had a daddy. What is one?

I fought alone even if all the love I gave feeling was fading farther from me. I try not to fall. But with a life I have lived, would you ever say more? I was that good-looking guy. Everyone Experience pain one way or another in their life this is why I write poetry of the nightmares I'm always in leaving me in the dark days with all the pain I have collected but always trying to be strong hoping for more good times because these feelings I can't feel and know there is no giving up knowing that there is no escaping or hiding in even if so many knows your name and see your pain and watch you fall but don't stop to catch you as your being watched in the rain and not being missed feeling everyone has left me here in pain hurting fighting cancer acting they didn't hear me even if I never changed rain or shine even

If I want to be found and trying to find my heart even if I need a ladder to climb to it I will never stop running to my dreams Regardless what people say, I can , And I will be something more.

All my life, I come from a low mid poor house with no father but 5 siblings and a mother trying to be daddy to try paying bills. I sat there watching her suffering a fight, raising me and my siblings for many younger years, as I'm learning off the streets, learning to be a leader, a boss in a teenage year pushing black bags of greens for many years. Having many working in my empire rising fast , until that day 3 days before my 21st birthday I got out Matched with nothing no one could ever save me Being real, I couldn't explain With this, it's killing me slowly Being hit by a semi losing everything I ever made was gone in the blink of an eye ,I was one of the first to walk with a high school degree in a damaged home with love apart And pain that made it work Being hit by a semi, I lost my career in football, I lost a sense of smell, and having cancer in my blood called PV bone morrow disease no cure but treat by taking blood every few weeks.

This happened in 2006. I was 20 years old and got shocked me for years until in 2021 when I was asked to go to Roswell Cancer for testing and finding out I had been sick for many years because a doctor never looked at the Symptoms but just give me antibiotics for years so when I was in the room and doctors told me, could I sit down "I look in their eyes and tell them no! Where I come from, we stand tall, never fall! As everyone leaves, I stand there trying not to fall, that day changed my life forever, waking me, showing me life's too short. You make your life the way you live it. So, I went home to teach myself how to read again and how to write again because I my memories fading having brain trauma from 2006.I'm in the arms of an angel, being scared of life without him not here being more than a close friend but my best friend, the Champaign MVP of this team. Now wishing could walk to heaven to bring him back home. Or wishing he has visiting hours, but knowing there's holes in the floors of heaven, and he can see me always. But it's a shame, he's not here he would be so proud of me. I promised him never to let go even if it's a harder fight. And all the fun has left and left even before what is the future I don't know; how will life be? And will never be the same and learn how to say goodbye, because some don't get second chances. With my walls, I built that's now crumbling, having a foundation falling apart, seeing no one wants to see me get anywhere and not holding no secrets heeled behind it, no one wants to see me succeed or go anywhere but fall on my face and not show up , but I keep getting up , with each day getting harder , being too late ,Being tired each second ticking by feeling I can't stop so tired of this pain, and I really mean it feeling it's lasting forever until my last breath, asking for more of such a prayer , so scared of life ,Knowing my health is at 40 30% I CAN'T STOP FIGHTING LIFE PROBLEMS, AND WILL NOT STOP EVEN IF LIFE KEEPS THROWING HAY MAKERS as I'M GETTING BACK UP , FOR THERE WILL BE NEVER NO PEACE IN THIS NIGHTMARE IM LIVING IN and this PAIN OF a BOX that's A HEART fading farther from me. I'm a secondary cancer fighter of PV bone morrow disease, I also fight seizures and depression for me losing.

My youngest brother and my oldest brother in a couple of years, I found out I've had cancer sense for over 15 years, and no doctor would listen until the one day a new doctor checked my red blood cells to tell me go to Roswell cancer Institute to be seen I stood up as Roswell doctors told me sit you can see it in my eyes, As I'm hurting praying for peace feeling it's never going stop until this heart freezes all over There's no prescription For this hurt, I realized it's getting late and tired of being in addiction to pain ....

I think, I've have, fallen again, I didn't want to, but I hope I'll be okay, and I'm Promising I'll do my best , As My PSTD is acting up again, I NEED YOU TO CATCH ME , EVERYONE HAS LEFT ME, I'm here alone. Now, THE GROUND IS WHERE I LAY, let me play my head here, I'm at the end, and now let's slow down, I promise I did my best.

You were like my best friend; I can't hide it anymore. You were more than a friend,

I couldn't tell you, now like where I am, this is where I lay my head now. Is it over? I Feel This Knife cutting deeper into my thoughts. To hope they are more likely than not over yet .I love you. Every day standing here in the rain, you were more than a friend missing you, my dear brother. I promise, I'm doing my best trying to be, but so hard I can't let go. I need your love more than ever hard when you're missing in this nightfall. I just can't, and I need you more than ever. I think I've fallen standing here in the rain with you missing. I'm a little off steady, so lost and a little confused, and i can't run from this pain. With this dim swift, deepening in my twilight throbbing heedless un calmed pushed stealthily alone, clinging intense Torturing life wringing deep affection lonely darkest path slender, mistresses dim moonlighting, clasped tightly anxiously low moan broke from her lips. Feeling lost thinking of how life is slipping away from my grasp, kissing the cross every night, no one knows my unconscious cry racing to the sky as blindly of all sights, with fearful breathless tainted chained in darkness folded up weakened sinking in deep frenzied drowning drenching of my own rain constancy with a shook heartbroken heavy with near death as I seemed of fallen begging for forgiveness I'm bleeding poison in each of my veins scattered obsession as my parched lips gripping As there's tears drops running breaking eyes lost wait feeling nothing will heal right trembling Burst into passionate tears Stripped lost in a maze of my 1000 days bitterness a unbearable solitary burden battle I'm living in by myself losing in A realization that I Have a foundation That was sinking more quick in this sand that I give you a permanent part of my heart. I am so sick hiding behind this fake smile, looking out my windows crying to my pillow, feeling hopeless this time it will never end feeling everybody I love walks away looking out my windows crying to my pillow sick of this thing praying but he treats me like shit it hurts, really fucking hurt feeling like nobody is around I'm sick of this Universe taking everything from me hiding behind this fake smile, I am sick of crying, hiding behind my smile until that day it doesn't change praying but to get bullshit. Having no help dying slowly inside with no time on my side, So, I need to speak before being out of time. I feel this will never be ok, so I'm sick of this bullshit. Looking out my windows crying, feeling the same, this will never change. Being so pissed how this universe took so much from me, you think I'm happy, but really, I'm walking with nothing but a fake smile having emptiness It's all fake so hard to understand why anyone doesn't want to be around, losing count how many times. Sorry if this is goodbye, so if this goodbye just knows, I tired hope we run into each other sometime down the line. I'm numbed and trying to listen to my heartbeat wishing could go back in time because you're the girl of my dreams built to love " listen to your heart , and) as when I first met you that night knowing I could be that changed man because your that perfect girl in my arms listen to that heartbeat because your that one special woman in my arms and that's how it should be , Knowing when I met you are that one when my... heart speaks girl you are my key to my heart the girl in my arms girl you are hard to find, This is fact the first time we met this was going last forever feeling this you are my diamond In my heart. As I sit in this cold room waiting for answers from my Leukemia Doctors at Roswell Cancer Institute, They explain how I have rare secondary cancer, a secondary meaning They don't know how I have or how I got, The type of cancer I have is polycythemia Vera A secondary that was explained that it's with me Intel my last days a bone morrow disease that has no cure but to treat by takings a Point of blood out as my red blood cells keep Cloning cells And it has no stopping but to keep on making more , it is a hard road. To be, on as I am young and scared to be, I have been fighting with this, polycythemia Vera is a dog fight. Someday, I feel I'm losing but I keep on getting back up and so far in two years Roswell has taken hundreds of points of blood from my body making me weaker than I ever can remember in this short life I have lived.......

Heaven Got Two Angels Tonight

It seems nothing will feel right. Heaven got two angels tonight, missing your smiles, it seems nothing will feel right. Heaven got two angels tonight, missing your smiles, I'm missing your laughter. Heaven got two angels tonight missing use tonight as I close my eyes. I dream about heaven tonight missing use tonight, seeing uses again as I dream of heaven tonight

It seems nothing will feel right. Heaven got two angels tonight, missing their smiles,

I'm missing your laughter. Heaven got two angels tonight missing use tonight as I close my eyes. I dream about heaven tonight. It feels like nothing isn't right as heaven took us from us, seeing how perishes life can be, it seems nothing will feel right. Heaven got two angels tonight, missing your smiles, and I'm missing your laughter. Heaven got two angels tonight missing use tonight as I close my eyes. I dream about heaven tonight missing use every moment you're not here.

www.ingramcontent.com/pod-product-compliance
Lightning Source LLC
LaVergne TN
LVHW012057070526
838200LV00070BA/1896